Saving God *from* Religion

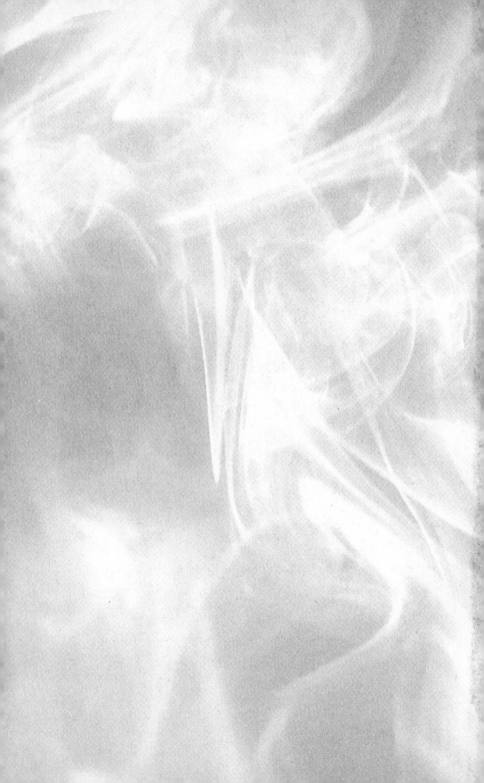

Saving God

from

Religion

A Minister's Search for Faith
in a Skeptical Age

Robin R. Meyers

Convergent
New York

All rights reserved.
Published in the United States by Convergent Books,
an imprint of Random House,
a division of Penguin Random House LLC, New York.
convergentbooks.com

CONVERGENT BOOKS is a registered trademark and its
C colophon is a trademark of Penguin Random House LLC.

Title page art from an original photograph by Thomas Picard.

ISBN 978-1-9848-2251-2
Ebook ISBN 978-1-9848-2252-9

Printed in the United States of America

Book design by Virginia Norey

10 9 8 7 6 5 4 3 2 1

First Edition

*This book is dedicated to
my three remarkable granddaughters,
Iris, Hazel, and Eleanora.
May we repair the future we have borrowed from them,
and pray for the healing of the earth with more than words.*

Contents

Saving God *from* Religion

Prologue

The Night God Fell
from the Ceiling

I was dozing through art history class in college when something woke me up and planted the seeds of a Big Dream. We were studying the magnificent frescoes of Michelangelo on the ceiling of the Sistine Chapel. The slides—that's what we used in those days—dropped into place as the Kodak carousel clicked around, humming with the white noise of the fan. My mind wandered as the professor described the chapel's creation. Many people think Michelangelo painted the frescoes on his back, he explained, but that's not true. Instead, the artist stood atop a rig of scaffolding, constructed specially for the occasion, craning his neck at the ceiling for hours just a few inches from his work. He complained often about the pain, about the fact that he was a sculptor, not a painter. Yet somehow he managed to achieve perspective without seeing his work from below. "A magnificent accomplishment," as the professor put it. My mind still wandered.

Michelangelo started painting in 1508, commissioned by Pope Julius II. The chapel, which often appears smaller than expected to the hordes of tourists, is built to the exact biblical dimensions of the Temple of Solomon on Jerusalem's Temple Mount. "Did anyone know this?" the professor asked. Silence. Lots of minds were wandering.

The lecture droned on. "It has always been the pope's private chapel. Along with frescoes by Botticelli, Perugino, and Pinturicchio, it is dominated at one end by *The Last Judgment*, which Michelangelo filled with nude males reportedly inspired by his visits to Rome's brothels. The nudes so offended subsequent popes that, in 1564, the Council of Trent demanded that the more 'prominent' nudes in *The Last Judgment* be made more decent, and the artist Daniele da Volterra was commissioned to paint underwear, or *braghe* (draperies), to cover them."

The mention of nudity stirred a few students to attention. "For a church that is based on the incarnation, the Word becoming flesh, we haven't been very good at loving the body," he continued. The class leaned forward.

That's when it happened. The last slide dropped into place, and the chapel's most famous painting appeared on the screen. *The Creation of Adam*. Perhaps the most replicated and parodied image of all time. In it, God appears as an elderly white and bearded man, wrapped in a swirling cloak. He reaches his right arm toward a reclining Adam, who is completely nude and reaching back—albeit half-heartedly. Their fingers do not quite touch.

In that *separation*, that small yet cosmic gap between God's finger and Adam's, Christian theology pitched its tent. People have wondered: Does the gap represent a divine spark that Adam has not yet received? Does it stand for the tragic separation between humans and God that is the root of all sin? Or is it the artist's rendering of the essential message of creation in Genesis 1:27: that humans, although lower than God, are made in God's image and likeness? I could not take my eyes off that "gap" and wondered what, if anything, could ever close it. "Mind the gap," I remembered hearing on a subway platform on the London Underground. But this was something deeper and more compelling than personal safety. As it turned out, this was the first stirring of a call to ministry. But that comes later.

Our professor turned to the class. "Look at the twelve figures surrounding God." He trained his pointer on one female figure in particular. "Who is that woman under God's arm?" More silence. "Is she Eve, gazing toward Adam and about to be offered as a gift? Is she the Virgin Mary or Sophia, the goddess of wisdom? We don't know because art historians are still arguing about this."

A young woman raised her hand, but when the professor called on her, she hesitated to speak and seemed almost embarrassed by what she was about to say. "I don't know the identity of the woman," she offered, "but I can't get over how buff God is."

"How *buff*?"

"Yes, he is old, but he's in great shape! Check out the arms. God must go to the gym. He's ripped." The class rippled with laughter. Then, for a few minutes, we all just stared at the image, and the power of it lingered.

"It was the Renaissance," the professor said, trying to recover. "The world had discovered the body to be beautiful, and in particular Michelangelo, who is widely believed to have been homosexual, drew and sculpted far more male nudes than female nudes."

"That's a shame," said a frat boy in the class. More laughter.

Then, just as the class was about to end, the professor pulled out a clipping from *The New York Times* and read it aloud:

> Dateline Rome—Pietro Bonatti, caretaker of the Vatican's Sistine Chapel and of the Pontifical Sacristy, died of a lung ailment in his Vatican apartment this morning. He was 83 years old. Following a four-century-long family tradition that started under Pope Sixtus V, Mr. Bonatti inherited the caretakership of the places of worship adjoining St. Peter's Basilica from his father, Antonio, who died in 1938. He served in that capacity under four Pontiffs, including Pope Paul VI, who named him "Gentleman of His Holiness" in 1963.[1]

There was a moment of awkward silence, after which the frat boy spoke for the class.

"And why are you telling us this?"

"Because," the professor replied, "it is important that you know that art is not just created—it is also preserved by caretakers. By people who sweep the floor, check the humidity in the room, and clean up after the crowds. It is their job to protect art from the millions of tourists whose skin and hair follicles flake off, rise to the ceiling, and coat the frescoes. Someone has to tell them to hush, to stop taking pictures, and finally to leave, especially the loud ones who are drunk. These caretakers are the only ones who see the art when no one else is in the room. The eyes in the paintings follow them on their silent rounds. They whisper their secrets in the darkness. What I am saying is that everyone knows the names of the artists, but no one ever knows the names of the caretakers. Now you do. His name was Pietro Bonatti."

The bell rang. We still had bells in those days, and I walked out of class thinking more about Pietro than about Michelangelo. Little did I know that many years later, this germinal idea would disturb my sleep in the form of a very strange dream. I had my life all planned out. I would get certified to teach high school English in some mythical classroom where all of the students were eager to learn. Except something else was tugging at me, something that was difficult to explain to my friends, much less to my fiancée.

One lazy afternoon, sitting alone in a tiny garage apartment studying for finals, I looked out the window at nothing in particular. A solitary bird was calling, but not to me. Something stirred. The world seemed at once both utterly indifferent and indescribably beautiful. As much as I loved literature, bigger questions were calling, some without any answers at all. So without hesitation, and with a kind of reckless disregard for a lifetime of consequences, I ditched the idea of teaching and decided to go to seminary.

When I got there, we talked a lot about dreams and their possible meanings. Not the kind Freud attributed to people's repressed desires, but the kind that makes a "thin place" between heaven and earth, between what is and what ought to be. Prophetic dreams, instructive dreams, apocalyptic dreams—the kinds many Christians believe are messages from

God. None of the dreams, however, were thought to be messages *about* God. That is, until one night I dreamed about my old art history class, and the forgotten lives of caretakers.

My dream was about Pietro's successor; let's call him Francesco. Every morning, he would grab a broom, look up at that image of God reaching out to Adam, and start sweeping the floor. He lived out his life doing this humble work beneath those masterpieces—beneath that gap between man and God.

One night, something terrible happened. It was four in the morning, and in the dream, I had become Francesco. I *was* the custodian of the Sistine Chapel, doing my rounds in another room, when a crash from the chapel jolted me awake. I dressed and ran into that sacred space, the room smelling of dust and plaster. And that's when I saw it. In a pile on the floor, in a thousand pieces, was all that remained of the most famous fresco in the world.

I looked up to the ceiling and saw a dark gash where the painting had been. Adam's reclining body remained, but his hand now stretched toward nothing. The plaster where Michelangelo's image of God and his heavenly host had been fixed for five hundred years had broken lose and fallen to the floor. God had fallen off the ceiling.

I looked in horror at the wreckage. *This can never be repaired*, I thought to myself. Then I realized that everyone was still asleep, so I sat alone in the chapel for a long time, looking up at the void and then down at the pile of rubble on the floor. Strangely, a verse came to mind that I'd never thought could apply to God. *Dust we are, and to dust we shall return.*

Just then, a gaggle of priests came wafting into the room,

their frantic voices babbling out a song of grief and indignation.

"Francesco, how could this happen?" one of them said, looking at me as if I were to blame.

"I am only the night watchman," I replied. "I heard the noise, just like you did, and came running."

"So what on earth could have caused this?" said a puffy, red-faced prelate—his crucifix resting almost horizontally atop an enormous belly.

In the silence that followed, I said the first thing that came to mind.

"Tired, perhaps?"

"Tired?" responded the portly priest, incredulous. "What on earth do you mean?"

I went back to sweeping up the broken pieces of God with a broom and thought for a moment about the irony of a church that has for so long talked about the "fall"—but only of man.

"Tired of being up there," I said. "Maybe even lonely?"

"Lonely!?" the big man bellowed.

"Look, you're a janitor, not a theologian," his assistant said. "This is just a structural failure, that's all—it's old plaster. We will put God back where he belongs."

"Maybe," I replied. "Or maybe that's not where he belongs."

I tried handing the dustpan and a spare broom to his assistant.

"Can I get some help here?"

The big priest looked incredulous. "Excuse me? It's not what we do."

"Well, you should try it. Because—"

"Because why?"

"Because God has always been down here."

Disclaimer of All Disclaimers

Dear reader, let's get the most obvious question out of the way. *Who writes a book about God?* An aging seminary professor in an ivory tower, perhaps? A theological narcissist who has God on speed dial? A hip young pastor who jots his sermons down on a pub napkin late Saturday night? Or is it perhaps one of those self-appointed coffee shop gurus who thinks she can prove the existence—or nonexistence—of God while waiting in line for a pumpkin spice latte?

Authors are told to write about what they know, which makes any book about God inherently absurd. We do not "know" God in the way that we know about other things, even though we often talk about God as if we did. Indeed most of us talk about the *mysterium tremendum et fascinans* (the transcendent mystery before which human beings tremble and are fascinated) as casually as we would talk about a next-door neighbor, a rich uncle, or a box of soap.

One of my seminary professors mused in class one day that clergy seem to think that chatting about God as if the two of them went "way back" was a sign of faith instead of a symptom of idolatry. Sermons are filled with God language that is so casual and familiar as to render the Almighty a kind of tourist attraction, not unlike a giant green bird sitting in the branches of a tiny tree in the preacher's backyard. Its enormous weight bends the sapling branches almost to the ground.

Whatever one thinks about, or feels, when the word "God" is spoken or written, the last association that should come to mind is the word "obvious." Perhaps it would be better to refrain from speaking the name of God at all, or to leave out the vowels when writing "YHWH" to show respect, as the rabbis did. Because let's face it, speaking of God as if He were a life coach or She were a BFF—or assuming that God has a gender to begin with—has not helped a dying church to catch another breath. I have wondered if the decline of organized religion has less to do with secular humanism and more to do with the suffocating way in which people of faith speak about that which they do not know.

When church attendance first started to wane, pundits claimed that liberal churches were shrinking because they were not sufficiently conservative, unambiguous, or doctrinal. But in the last decade, the Southern Baptists have lost more than a million members.[2] The fact is that organized religion of almost every stripe is declining and graying across the board. It's an equal-opportunity disappearing act, and it's complicated, except for one universal thread. The *young* are leaving religion in droves. Four out of ten younger millennials (eighteen to twenty-nine) are "nones" (no religious affiliation). That is four times higher than it was in 1980. "In fact, the fastest-growing religion in America is . . . no religion at all."[3] Today there are clergy who confess to hearing a very strange question from people considering membership: "Can I join your church even though I'm an atheist?"

Against this backdrop, writing a book about God is literary presumption on a cosmic scale. The subject matter is both the most important and the most impossible. Yet the world has changed so much since the days of Michelangelo that a new conversation about God is long overdue. Our discussion in this book will not be couched in the familiar (and often hypocritical) dichotomy of religious versus secular fundamentalists. We will be looking for what Catherine Keller calls a "third way." Something that preserves the mystery by knowing better than to call it one.

To begin, here's what we did not know when human beings first began worshipping what we now call God. Our best guess is that the universe is thirteen to fourteen billion years old, and our beloved earth is but a tiny, fertile outpost in the suburbs of a minor galaxy—what the late astronomer Carl Sagan called "a pale blue dot." Then there is dark matter, and black holes, and something called M-theory, a shadowy concept posited to lie at the end of a mathematical labyrinth known as superstrings. In short, the age of science has given us a lot to feel very small and humble about.

Even so, this has not changed our capacity to practice spiritual pride or turn the Mystery of Mysteries into a kind of cosmic bellhop. We don't mean to diminish the idea of the holy, the transcendent, and the numinous. But in our desire to capture and express this mystery, we talk about God as if we had written God's job description. We make God the default explanation for almost everything that happens, the good stuff and the stuff that horrifies us, even if those claims make no sense at all. Much of this language assumes that God is like the CEO of creation, running the universe from a celestial throne before which mere mortals cringe in fear and supplication.

Even so, we are hesitant to challenge our assumptions

about God, because, after all, faith is such a deeply personal thing. Who are we to question it or express our frustration over it? We admit that we are all walking around a mountain too high to climb, so we just freeze up, or look away, or change the subject when our friends and loved ones tell us matter-of-factly what God is up to, whom God has chosen, and which side of the latest bloody war God is on. Just listen to the soundtrack of our prayers or the elevator music of our culture.

God chatter is ubiquitous, based on unchallenged assumptions that the featherless bipeds on this pale blue dot are really the apple of God's eye; favorite children in the infinite darkness; even the recipients of partisan favors to help our favorite sports team win the big game. God has a personality, of course, because we do. And the eternally durable image is that of a strict father trying to control wild kids, not unlike the "great and powerful Oz"—all special effects and no soul.

The real unchallenged assumption is that God is an agent who is busy doing things, *acting* in human history to honor and reward those who worship correctly and believe the right things, while punishing those who don't. Indeed the Western Christian God is a heavenly vending machine. We deposit our prayers, push the right doctrinal buttons, and wait for something we want to drop down. If the prize is not forthcoming, we may shake the machine, curse God, or be told by the preacher that we must "deposit" more faith.

What we can no longer deny, however, is that organized religion has a God crisis on its hands. Traditional theism, the idea that God is a kind of superperson who dwells outside the world as we know it and occasionally intervenes to answer prayers or impose the divine will, has run its course and been rejected by millions. To an entire generation of disillusioned young people, and millions who came before them, the God spoken about in church has become little more than a projection of human hopes and fears. We need new ways to conceive of being human. New ways to be in relationship to the sacred and to one another.

A Different Kind of Book

So this will be a different kind of book. I will not attempt to persuade you that God exists, does not exist, or cannot be known to exist in the same way that your cat does. Instead, it will be a collection of *stories* told by a parish minister after a lifetime of listening and learning from people who are struggling to believe.

There is no more painful moment in parish ministry than to see a lost soul come to church looking for mercy, only to find legalism. My father once told me a story about the insanity of his denomination's insistence that no one goes to heaven who hasn't been baptized—and baptized by full immersion. A young man he knew had Lou Gehrig's disease. It had progressed to the point that it was impossible for him to walk, much less get baptized. He was terrified that, having not been baptized, he would go to hell. My father told him that no loving God would punish anyone in his situation, and to rest assured that he was loved and accepted.

As the man neared death, however, a traveling evangelist came to town and told him that there are no exceptions, even hinting that his disease must be a form of punishment for sin. "You must be baptized if you want to see your loved ones in heaven," he told the young man, "and we can make it happen." Hospital staff were asked to bring in a giant mechanical sling that would lift his ravaged body above a large tank of water and slowly lower him down. As he screamed in pain, the evangelist spoke the magic words, and the young man was baptized. Later, as he lay exhausted in his bed and weeping, the evangelist told him that all the pain was worth it, and that now he could better understand the suffering of Jesus. "Rest assured that your reservation in heaven is ready, and that you will be given a new body as well."

Such stories raise the question: How does religion survive its own practitioners? Is it because we are all hardwired to seek transcendence? Is it because we can't help but wonder where we came from, where we are going, and to Whom or to What we belong? Either way, I believe our choice is not between orthodox beliefs about God on one hand and radical nihilism on the other. The choice is between one view of divinity as expressed by religious orthodoxy and many others that are emerging now in the age of science and spiritual hunger. *This book is written for everyone who is struggling with the old and narrow definitions of God but has yet to see any coherent and comprehensive way to reimagine the Ultimate Mystery.*

This will not be easy. Those of us who grew up in the church still carry old and beautiful words in the backs of our throats. Some of them feel like orphans now, not to mention the ideas that go with them. We need to redefine them, or swallow them and form new ones, because we long for a faith that is more than judgmental certainty, more than "believe and receive." In a world where everything is entangled, woven into what Dr. Martin Luther King, Jr., called a "seamless garment of destiny," we are hungry for new ways to heal and transform the broken world we inhabit.

This project comes at a critical moment in human history. We are a species headed for extinction, the first generation to know the truth about global climate change and the last to have a chance to do anything about it. This is not just a political crisis; it is a theological one. Our ancient longing for a supreme leader in heaven mirrors itself in our choice of worldly leaders. We may hate what Daddy dishes out, but in the end we have been conditioned to believe that it must be good for us—because, in the words of the 1950s sitcom, father knows best.

Grown men have approached me after a sermon on the parable of the Prodigal Son to say that their fathers never once said, "I love you, son." Women have confessed that their appearance was so critical to their self-image that they spent years battling depression and eating disorders. Each time they walked past the window displays at Victoria's Secret, they were confused about the true meaning of the word "angel." Our conspicuous consumption, our mindless consumerism, our "enough is never enough" idolatry, causes us to fashion a God of the so-called prosperity gospel—a God who shows his love for us by making us rich—even though the real message in the Bible is that wealth is spiritually debilitating.

The deep, dark secret of organized religion is that abusive earthly fathers have often compromised the idea of a Heavenly Father, handing down the teaching of a God who loves us but is also perpetually *disappointed* in us. This divinely inspired shame has made it impossible for millions of followers to love themselves. Would a Heavenly Mother be better? Depends. Perhaps it is the very idea of a *personal* God that is most in need of revision. Something beyond gender and gerrymandering altogether. Perhaps something that is not "out there" so much as "in here." What Paul Tillich called a God of the depths instead of a God of the heights.

At least this much is now clear. Marketing an old God with better signage and parking won't work. Offering classes in Christian aerobics (whatever that is, exactly) won't work. Preaching about "muscular Christianity" (whatever that is, exactly) won't work. Turning the gospel upside down, claiming that wealth is a sign of God's favor (instead of a spiritual hazard), won't work. So where do we begin?

To put it plainly, we need to stop looking up—at a God who lives on the ceiling, directing and pronouncing judgment upon everything below—and start *looking around*.

1

Made in the Image of Humans

*How can an infinitesimal part of the universe understand
the whole? We are drops of water trying
to understand the sea.*

—WILL DURANT

The phone call came late, and every pastor knows what that means. The voice at the other end was both frantic and forlorn. I recognized my parishioner immediately, calling me with news about her niece.

"She's lost another baby," she said.

"A miscarriage?" I replied, fearing something even worse.

"No, the little boy is dead in her womb. She is six months along. They will induce labor in the morning, and she wants you to baptize the baby." She gave me the room number, and I repeated it back, because by then she had started to cry.

It was the mother's second stillbirth—both boys. I had performed a kind of funeral service for the first one, an early miscarriage, and then she had had two healthy girls. Now a second boy had died in her womb, this one a viable fetus. Apparently, in some rare instances, the presence of a Y chromosome causes the mother's body to reject the fetus as it would a foreign object. Who knows why? Who ever knows why? But as I put on my shoes and walked out to my car, I knew that was exactly what the mother would ask me. *Why?*

I'm a preacher. I don't often find myself at a loss for words, but there are some important things they don't teach you in seminary. For starters, no one taught me to how to baptize a dead baby. To be honest, no one taught me how to baptize a living one either, but you figure these things out. You dip your fingers in the font, make the sign of the cross on the baby's forehead, and recite the baptismal formula. Then you do the most important thing. You pose for family photos. Chances are no one remembers what you said anyway, but one thing is certain: It is a joyful occasion.

I have always taken the infant in my arms and spoken to the child, letting the parents and the congregation overhear. But on this day, there would be no adoring congregation, no flowers, and no sunlight streaming into the sanctuary. Nothing I had said before would work. This mother was about to deliver a tiny corpse. She would never nurse it or rock it to sleep, never hold its warm and scented head against her cheek. What was I supposed to say when I walked into the room? *Got any ideas, Reverend? Remember, you represent a God of love and justice.*

The mother asked that I come after the delivery, so that a photographer could take pictures of her dead son to share on Facebook. I was having a hard time imagining this, but it is not my job to judge what brings comfort, only to bring more. I rehearsed some lines in the hospital elevator, but they all sounded hollow. *Will she want a baptismal certificate?* I won-

dered. *Of course she will, and you forgot to bring one.* I made a
note to fill it out later, using the full given name of the deceased.

At least I remembered to bring the chalice to hold the
water. It was the same silver bowl that I have used for all the
baptisms I have performed over thirty-five years serving
the same church. It was also the same chalice I had used to
baptize the mother. When I opened the door, she looked up
and recognized it immediately.

"Oh good, you brought the chalice."

I stepped into the room and looked into a tiny crib next to
her bed. There he was—smaller than a doll and dark purple,
the color of eggplant. He looked like a tiny wax figure, dressed
in a tiny baptismal outfit with a tiny crocheted stocking cap
on his head.

"Isn't he beautiful?" she said. "Isn't he perfect?"

I decided that silence was the best response, but that silence became unbearable for the mother's father. Standing
near the foot of the bed, he made a crude political joke about
Hillary Clinton. I did not laugh. *Why is it that human beings
have so much trouble with silence?* I wondered. Isn't that the
only response to such a moment? The baby's father was also
in the room, his head cupped in his hands. A second stillborn
son. In his mind, he had already signed the boy up for Little
League.

At that point, I did something I had never done before. I
picked up the chalice and asked for the full given name of a
dead baby. In unison, Mom and Dad spoke his first, middle,
and last names. I dipped my fingers into the chalice, filled out
of habit with warm water (because that's what living babies

prefer). I then pushed up the tiny stocking cap and placed my fingers on the baby's cold, lifeless forehead.

My fingers traced the sign of the cross on inert flesh. "I baptize you in the name of the Father, and of the Son, and of the Holy Spirit. Amen."

When I looked up, I saw the grandfather crying. This was no joke.

The God Problem

I left the room full of sadness and questions that wouldn't go away. If the ritual brought comfort to the family, then wasn't that reason enough to baptize a dead baby? My gut said yes—but infant baptism is a covenant between the living and the future. The parents promise that they will practice unconditional love in the way we are told God loves us. So what does it mean to baptize a baby whom no one will raise? Surely no God worthy of worship would wait on such a ritual to decide the baby's fate. I could not bring the child back to life, so *from what* was he being cleansed, and *to what* was he being restored?

I walked out of the hospital and into the light of a perfect September morning. It was Indian summer in Oklahoma. My car was parked in the spot reserved for clergy, because in this deeply evangelical state, we still enjoy special privileges. But in my mind, the God questions would not stop. I know countless clergy who ask these questions in the privacy of their minds but never admit it to anyone. What had I just done, and why had I done it?

It is not uncommon for ministers to say something like this to a mother who has lost her child: "I know you are devastated, but believe me, God had a plan for your little one. Maybe God wanted her in heaven early, to be with the angels." Really? Who could say such a thing? Those who believe in original sin would explain that even a stillborn baby needs forgiveness. If I believed this, I would immediately turn in my ministerial credentials and get a real job. It gives new meaning to the idea that we would be better off without religion.

I attended a funeral once that included a "viewing" at the end of the service. This is the peculiar and very expensive ritual that makes a dead person look alive—sleeping, perhaps. "So natural," the mourners say. As the family passed by the open casket, the minister was asked to say a few words of comfort. He looked at the widow and said, "Aren't you glad that your husband has gone to be with Jesus?" Without hesitation, she looked up and made eye contact so intense it resembled a laser. Then she said, "No. No, Reverend, I'm *not* glad. I would much prefer that he was still here, with me and the girls. Is Jesus going to pay the rent?"

In Oklahoma, we watch the sky for tornadoes, and when they drop down like ropes of death, they are truly terrifying. In the town of Moore, where tornadoes occur so frequently that the town could be mistaken for a kind of bowling alley for twisters, most people do not have basements. So when the sirens wail, and that roar "like a freight train" is heard, terrified parents will crawl into the bathtub with their children and pull a mattress over them—holding the straps as tightly as they can while their house explodes around them. Recently, the news media reported something too painful to imagine.

During one such tornado, an infant was sucked from her mother's arms because she could not hold on to her baby tightly enough. The little girl was found a quarter mile away, wrapped in a tree like so much storm debris. Later, when a preacher dropped by to comfort the mother, he said what he thought he was supposed to say, instead of just saying nothing. It was yet another version of this twisted idea that God calls some people home early and they are now in a "better place."

I do not know how the mother responded, but if someone said that to me, I would need to be physically restrained. If clergy are going to continue such theological malpractice, they should probably be accompanied by law enforcement.

As I near the end of my career as a parish minister, I can't help but think of what it means to be ordained and charged with speaking truth to power in America at a time like this. Our God language has remained essentially unchanged for thousands of years, even as the world has changed dramatically around us. In sermon after sermon, we speak of God's love for us as constant and unconditional, but then try to explain tragedy in ways that make God seem utterly capricious, even incomprehensibly cruel. A man confessed to me once that as a child he loved to sing, "He's Got the Whole World in His Hands."

"It was enormously comforting," he said, thinking of God holding the world in his cupped hands. "Until I got old enough to discover that he frequently drops it."

One of the problems with God talk is that any claim made about God is impossible to refute, much less prosecute.

Human courts at least have laws against libel. Theologians enjoy total immunity. If you say God did something, who can disprove it? If you say God talks to you, who can deny it? If you claim to be God's chosen people, all you have to do is reference your sacred scriptures, and sure enough, God is in the land-grant business.

Although it may sound strange, our deep desire to honor God may in fact be dishonoring God, not to mention making it impossible for millions to believe in God. If this God we honor is a God of unconditional love, but also responsible for everything that happens, then this must include dead babies, genocide, the scourge of sexual abuse, and the destruction of the only planet we have. Instead of advising the faithful that good things are "God's gift" but terrible things are "a mystery," perhaps we should try imagining God in entirely new ways. Instead of a God who delivers the good, the bad, and the ugly, *why can't we evolve into creatures who can separate the tragedies that result from purely physical forces in the natural world from the spiritual consequences of our own moral choices?* Instead of second-guessing the agency of God, why don't we turn our attention to what we can see and understand, namely the world in which we actually live, and a new *theology of consequence?*

Cause and effect have long been relegated to the world of science and logic, but seldom have we explored "consequentiality" as a deeply spiritual phenomenon. Instead of a remote God upon which we project our hopes and fears, we might find ourselves once again grounded in the mystery of what author and theologian Barbara Brown Taylor has called the

Luminous Web.[1] What if everything really is connected to everything else? What if we do indeed live in a world of spiritual as well as physical equilibrium?

Thanks to the blessing that is science, especially quantum physics, we now understand the nature of reality itself differently. A choice is now before us. We can continue to worship a God created in a pre-scientific cosmology that no longer exists, or we can graduate to an understanding of God that is as complicated and mysterious as the universe itself. In the process, we might move from fear to reverence. From obedience to wisdom. From separation to unity.

Tornadoes certainly look and sound evil. But in reality, they are just one of the strange and deadly shapes that clouds can get themselves into. The faithful response is to make sure your neighbors can share your storm shelter when the sirens blow. As for the real presence of God, it shows up when neighbors show up after the storm—to clean up, bring food, give money, donate blood, open their homes, and adopt orphans.

So lest we get ahead of ourselves, we should step back first and begin at the beginning. The best place to start is with the God impulse itself. Where did it come from? How did it evolve? Where has it taken us? Why is it now betraying us?

First Questions

Before language, before cave painting, before the making of any artifacts that could be left as evidence, some early human ancestor must have wondered if all that he could see was animated by a universal spirit that he could not see. Or it might have been a she who first wondered, if she could get anyone to listen. Whoever it was, and whenever this happened, *a longing for transcendence* hatched in the human heart and started us on the road to believing in God. We are here, so who made us? We feel pain and pleasure, so who wired us in that way? We have a tribal chief to lay down the law, so why not a heavenly one?

Maybe it was at the end of a long day of hunting and gathering when a bone-tired Neanderthal cousin sat poking at the fire—his deep-set dark eyes tucked under a sloping skull, watching the embers float up and flame out against a night sky littered with stars and streaked by comets. The world felt at once dangerous, fantastic, and incomprehensible. He had no idea why survival itself should take every waking moment and so often fail. She could not understand why babies are sometimes born dead.

The natural world baffled and frightened our ancestors. One day it rained too much, and the floods would come. The next day it rained too little, and drought turned the fields to dust. *Who has sewn the heavens shut?* The earth would crack, plagues would ravage an entire village, and their kindred would waste away. Snakes and scorpions crawled into the caves at night to bite children while they slept. A father would wake to the sound of a wailing mother who had found her little ones curled into cold lumps, their tiny eyes fixed in lifeless stares, their innocent mouths wide open.

The tribal elder lay down next to the fire one evening. He did not understand growing old, but pain was a nightly visitor. Just before he fell asleep, he must have wondered: *Why do these bones wither? Why does my eyesight grow dim? What does it mean that I can no longer run? What good is an old man, or an old woman, in a tribe that must hunt and gather to survive?*

My point is this: The horizontal world—that of our ancestors' daily experience—was full of pain and sorrow, and so the first place humans looked for help was "up." Perhaps some other world was out there that was not like this one. A world without pain and suffering, a world of plenty, a world of justice. Perhaps the first pair of hands even came together in a sign of desperation. *Please. If anyone or anything is out there, we could use some help down here.*

In short, we must have asked Einstein's famous question long before the frumpy genius did: *Is the universe a friendly place or not? It certainly does not appear to be. My tribe is never safe. We fall ill and die from diseases whose origins are invisible but whose victims haunt our sleep with their howling. Are they possessed by demons? Are they being punished for something they did or did not do? Is this the will of some invisible giant, a god of fertility, the lord of the hunt? Whatever it is, does it have anything to do with us? Is it a trickster or an assassin? Do we hide from it, or seek its face and beg its favor?*

To consider where the idea of God came from, and where it is going, we have to begin with questions. When did human consciousness evolve far enough to become self-aware about the meaning, value, and purpose of our actions and the things that happen to us?

In other words, when did our ancestors begin asking the ethical and existential questions that we still ask today? *May I take whatever I want from someone weaker than me? What does it mean to say that something belongs to me and not to someone else? Do I exist only as part of the tribe, or do I exist alone? Who or what is rewarding me one minute and punishing me the next? Am I any different from the animals around me, or by walking upright have I become the favored one?*

There must have also come a moment when the first humans began to wonder about the meaning of physical space, and the difference between the visible and the invisible. *Here is what I can see. Over there is something I can't make out clearly. And farther away I see nothing, even though I know that something is there.* How long was it before humans began to imagine the invisible and use symbols to fill in the blanks? *If my tribe lives here, and their tribe lives there, then who or what lives neither here nor there but everywhere? Why is the lightning visible but the thunder invisible? Is that a god clearing his throat? Like the wind, is there a spirit whose effects can be seen but whose shape is hidden? If we are defeated in battle, is it the work of some invisible warrior, and if so, how do I win his favor and avoid his wrath?* When did the human brain get big enough to start asking human questions? *Why am I here? Who made the earth and the sky? Does it matter whether I live or die? Are there spirit forces that I can enlist for battle, for food, for safety, for healing, for moral order?*

We don't know, and we will never know. But it is safe to say that before there were statues, before there were rituals, before the gods were named and turned loose in heaven to play their cosmic games, there were questions. And before the questions, someone *looked up after looking around.* In this simple, timeless move, we were given the gods. How many? Exactly as many as you need to explain why everything happens, or doesn't happen.

First Answers

The world of human experience is horizontal, particular, and limited. We see nothing beyond the horizon. But over time we realized that the horizon is not the end of things, but merely the limit of our sight. So how did the earliest humans first begin to relate to that which is beyond perception and comprehension? When did we begin to think that the gods we made in our own image could be bargained with? When did we first start calling on them, flattering them, making graven images to them, and pleading our case in ritual, song, and story?

We have evidence to suggest that long before *Homo sapiens* arrived, our Neanderthal relatives were reverently burying their dead with rituals that anticipated some kind of journey. These prehuman ancestors oriented the bodies of their deceased kindred in a certain direction and included tools and other items needed in the next life. Where did they think they were going? Who or what did they think would be there to receive them?

Perhaps 50,000 to 100,000 years ago, our ancestors went through a number of changes, going from prehuman to fully human. The markers were clear. We became self-aware, developed a moral sense, created and valued communities, and over time became more precise about our use of symbols and communication than any other species. But surely it was the knowledge of our own death that created what Sigmund Freud call "the trauma of self-consciousness" and theologian Paul Tillich called "the shock of nonbeing." This made *Homo sapiens* different from all other animals. "To be human is to experience self-consciousness, to know separation, to be made aware of limits and to contemplate ends," Tillich writes. "One cannot be human, therefore, without being filled with chronic anxiety."[2]

Such is the "blessing" of higher consciousness. Humans are separated from other animals by their ability to reason instead of acting only on instinct. Dogs bark, but they do not reflect on the nature of their barking. Animals go off to die, but they do not lie awake at night worrying about it. What's more, human infants remained helpless for a very long time and had to be taught the accumulated wisdom of the tribe. So we became both highly social creatures and chronically anxious ones.

As soon as humans began to understand cause and effect, wisdom was born. It may be impossible to know what will happen to us from one minute to the next, but we can certainly improve our odds for safety and survival. Tell stories. Make rules. Then teach the children. If one of them wants to know where such wisdom came from, tell them to look up.

Prior to the development of organized religion, some indigenous peoples believed that everything in the natural world, including inanimate objects, possessed a spiritual essence. Sir Edward Burnett Tylor coined the term "animism" (from the Latin *anima*, "breath, spirit, life") in his 1871 book, *Primitive Culture*. He defined animism as "the general doctrine of souls and other spiritual beings in general."[3] Whether or not animism was the first religion, it surely set the stage for both polytheism and monotheism. Once you imagine a world that is humming with spiritual energy, the next question is obvious: Are these animating spirits benevolent or demonic?

Whichever it was, these gods "were assumed to be personal, to have selfhood, to be in charge of their particular area of life, to be capable of responding to human need and to be in possession of supernatural powers."[4]

As it turns out, the idea that the gods were made in the image of humans is not a modern one, but is noted by the major Jewish prophets of the sixth century B.C.E. Amos, Micah, Nahum, and Isaiah all claim that the gods of those who had conquered Israel and forced her into exile were manufactured by humans. The first Greek critics of religion followed the prophets in questioning the traditional Olympian religion. They even brought some of the gods to trial, accusing them of heresy. Some of the philosophers had already begun searching for a single rational principle at the heart of the universe and dismissed the mythical role of the gods in shaping events. Xenophanes, a poet-philosopher from Ionia (570–478), questioned whether natural causes lie behind supposedly divine phenomena and noted that the gods were often depicted according to local conceptions of human attributes:

> *Ethiopians make their gods snub-nosed and black; the Thracians make theirs blue-eyed and red-haired. . . . Mortals imagine that the gods are begotten, and that the gods wear clothes like their own and have language and form like the voice and form of mortals.*[5]

The Athenian playwright-poet Critias (460–403), who wrote *Sisyphus*, theorized that men created the gods in order to frighten the wicked even if they acted, spoke, or thought in secret. "There is, he said, a spirit enjoying endless life, hearing and seeing with his mind, exceeding wise and all-observing, bearer of a divine nature. He will hear everything spoken among men and can see everything that is done."[6]

This idea that God is an eye in the sky that never sleeps persists to this day in both our religious and our cultural language. Even Santa Claus carries on this idea of God as the odd watcher, the eternal eye in the sky who never blinks: "He sees you when you're sleeping / He knows when you're awake / He knows if you've been bad or good / So be good for goodness' sake." To be honest, it is hard to imagine a creepier idea than this, especially for a teenager.

As scientists have begun to unravel the genetic source of religion, the so-called DNA of faith, many neuroscientists have come to believe that God is hardwired into the brain; that we possess a kind of "biology of belief," or what researchers refer to as a "neurology of transcendence."[7] Others say that God can be explained as a kind of psychological trait that aided natural selection. Religious systems helped our ancestors work effectively in small groups that survived and reproduced.

At the heart of this evolution theory is the notion that human beings are born with a powerful need for *attachment*. Survival itself is dependent upon protectors, beginning with our mothers. This attachment is reinforced physiologically through brain chemistry, and we remain hardwired to need protectors long after reaching adulthood. Soldiers will often cry out to their mothers as they lie dying, and all pastors have witnessed this same phenomenon when making hospital visits. At least one theory for the idea of God is that human beings transfer the permanent need for protectors to authority figures of any sort, including religious figures who presume to speak for, work for, and make available the power of the ultimate parent, God.

Is it any wonder that when the Judeans solidified their idea of one God, Yahweh, they wrote a creation myth—Genesis 3—that explained why a perfect God is not responsible for an imperfect creation? After Eve partakes of the forbidden fruit and supposedly plunges the whole world into sin, God hands down a sentence that not only shifts the blame to human beings but explains the fate they now deserve:

> To the woman he said, "I will greatly increase your pangs in childbearing; in pain you shall bring forth children, yet your desire shall be for your husband, and he shall rule over you." And to the man he said, "Because you have listened to the word of your wife, and have eaten of the tree about which I commanded you, 'You shall not eat of it,' cursed is the ground because of you; in toil you shall eat of it all the days of your life; thorns and thistles it shall bring forth for you; and you shall eat the plants of the field. By the sweat of your face you shall eat bread until you return to the ground, for out of it you were taken; you are dust, and to dust you shall return. (Genesis 3:16–19, New Revised Standard Version)

This creation myth (the second of two distinct and irreconcilably different accounts in Genesis) is the foundation upon which Western theology is built. To explain the world as it is now, we placed the blame squarely on the first humans and their original disobedience. We were given a test, and we flunked it. Eve does not come out of the story looking good, but God is off the hook, and the seeds of original sin are planted here. It is also the first case of the victimhood mentality. Adam blames the woman, who blames the snake.

In the description of God's visitation, walking in the garden in the cool of the evening, one is reminded of when a parent visits your room and you know you are in trouble. After the "talk," God returns to heaven (or wherever it is God comes from), and we are left to feel shame for our disobedience and wonder how best to avoid the wrath of an absent Father in the future.

This idea—that God is "up" and that hell is "down"—is a default setting in the human brain, and it has strongly influenced modern-day faith. We "lift" our voices in praise. In everyday religious conversation we are counseled to "talk to the man upstairs." Even when we bow our heads, we imagine that our prayers go not down, but up and out. Down has other connotations, and they are not divine.

In the Judeo-Christian tradition the psalmist sings, "I will lift up mine eyes unto the hills, from whence cometh my help" (Psalms 121:1, King James Version). Why look to the hills? Why not the plains or even the valleys? Isaiah counsels us, "Lift up your eyes and look to the heavens" (Isaiah 40:26, New International Version). The heavens are the abode of the Almighty (or before monotheism, the playground of the gods), and religious figures were said to have "gone up" on a mountain to receive God's revelation before they "came down" to deliver and interpret it to mere mortals below. When the scriptures speak of "no God above God" the prize is vertical. Our lives are horizontal, but our deities must be higher. Their vantage point is surely a cosmic tower where they can watch their subjects below.

This also makes perfect sense for human beings who first conceived of the gods by looking around at their daily existence. Everything we experience on earth is arranged in a vertical hierarchy of power. Larger animals prey on smaller ones, often from "above," where they watch their prey below and then swoop down. The larger, more powerful animal slays the smaller, less powerful ones—standing "over" their kill. In battle, the tallest warriors are the most intimidating, and if one human seems wiser and more powerful than the others, he is "raised up" to rule "over" his subjects as a monarch, and then he "hands down" his edicts from "on high." Surely "up" is more powerful than "down," and the former is where any self-respecting god would live.

In the Hebrew scriptures, the story of the Tower of Babel (Genesis 11:1–9) depicts those "below" trying to access those in heaven "above." Not only does the punishment (confused tongues) serve to explain why humans speak so many different languages, but it also reminds us that if one is trying to get into heaven, one does not excavate, one *elevates*. Ours is still a sky God living somewhere above the clouds. This "verticality" in religion has scarcely been challenged in our time, despite quantum physics and string theory. We still look up after looking around.

Knowledge Is Not Redemptive

A familiar teaching from the life of Jesus is his warning not to put new wine in old wineskins. "No one sews a piece of unshrunk cloth on an old cloak; otherwise, the patch pulls away from it, the new from the old, and a worse tear is made. And no one puts new wine into old wineskins; otherwise, the wine will burst the skins, and the wine is lost, and so are the skins; but one puts new wine into fresh wineskins" (Mark 2:21–22, NRSV).

This parable has been interpreted in many ways, but in its original context it surely had something to do with the futility of trying to *become* something new while still "contained" in (or by) something old. No doubt the parable, which appears in all three synoptic gospels (Matthew, Mark, and Luke), reflects the quarrels between this new sect of Judaism and her elders, the keepers of her tradition. As the specter of the approaching divorce grew larger, it was no doubt useful to cite this parable to express the frustration of trying to be a "new" creation in an "old" religious system. Perhaps a complete break from the past is needed, from tradition, from "old wineskins."

I have heard LGBTQ youth interpret this parable as a reminder that gender and sex are not the same thing, and that a human being can actually be born into the "wrong" body. In a similar way, those who make a break with religious orthodoxy often speak of "knowing what they cannot un-know." Once a new religious paradigm settles into the heart, and faith becomes a new way of *being* in the world, not a belief system with postmortem rewards or punishments, the mind also crosses the Rubicon.

Knowing the truth and then falling away from it (apostasy) is considered the worst sin of all. But there is another way to be unfaithful, a kind of apostasy in reverse. What happens when we grasp a *new* truth and then refuse to embrace it out of fear that an old truth is being rejected, along with the institutions and loved ones that still hold it? This is precisely the dilemma we face when it comes to God.

I will never forget a story that one of my seminary professors told in class one day. He had agreed to be acting dean for fifteen months. He said it felt like fifteen years.

One day, his executive assistant knocked on the door and said, "There's someone here to see you."

"OK, please ask her to come in."

She was a middle-aged woman whose face was etched by pain. Her first question was simple and straightforward. "Are you the dean?"

"Yes, ma'am, I am."

"Is that the highest position in the seminary?"

"Yes, ma'am, I suppose it is," the professor replied.

"Good. I need you to do something for me." She motioned for him to follow her and led him out of the building and into the parking lot. She stopped beside her car and opened the back door. Slumped in the backseat was her younger brother, who had been a senior at the University of Oklahoma. He had been in a terrible car wreck and was now in a coma. His eyes were fixed, and his chin was covered in drool.

"For eight months he has been like this," she said.

"I'm so sorry," the professor replied.

She had quit her job as a schoolteacher to take care of him. All her money was gone. She was too proud to ask for help, but she had nothing left. She opened the door a little wider and asked the professor to lean in a little closer. "He knows that you are here," she said.

Then she looked the professor right in the eye. "I'd like for you to heal him."

The professor said, "I can pray for him. And I can pray with you. But I do not have the gift of healing."

She got behind the wheel and started the engine. Then she rolled down the window and looked at the professor as her eyes filled with tears.

"Then what in the world do you do?"

And she drove away.[8]

Because I was training for ministry when I heard this story, I could not get the woman's question out of my head. *Then what in the world do you do?* If you can't deliver a miracle. If you can't ease someone's pain. If you can't throw away anybody's crutches. If you can't pluck that dead baby from the tree after the tornado and breathe the breath of life back into her and then hand her back to her mother, then *what do you do*, and why do you need a God license to do it? The money isn't that good. The hours are terrible (pastors never get to clock out). The social status disappeared with the 1950s. The rate of burnout, dropout, or nervous breakdown is higher than for any other profession. So what in the world *do* you do, and *why* do you do it?

Strange as it sounds, God only knows. Not the God we have created in our own image. Not the deity that arose when we divided the cosmos into a false binary called the *absolute* and the *dissolute*—the former of which is the desire for absolute certainty, reacting against the fear of the latter, "a nihilistic dissolution, a relativism indifferent to meaning and morality."[9] Perhaps there is another way.

Western Christianity has long turned on the axis of sin and salvation and is marketed to individuals as a product. Faith's relationship to rewards reinforces the idea that the spiritual life is a competition with winners and losers—just like everything else in a capitalist society. Jesus came with a product (salvation) and delivered it on the cross (substitutionary atonement) for the ultimate postmortem reward (heaven).

This approach to religion, which is still the dominant approach, means that faith is *transactional* instead of *relational*. Being "saved" is just another zero-sum game (you know you have won because others have lost). Yet nothing in our scriptures points to enlightenment as a transaction. On the contrary, it means an awakening: "scales falling from our eyes." For Christians, this means that Jesus of Nazareth is both a real human being and a universal or cosmic Christ. Richard Rohr reminds us that Christ is not Jesus's last name but a recognition that the human and the divine could be united in space and time—in the actual, present world that we inhabit. Because his followers saw him as the incarnation of this mystical union, Jesus threatened our world, in which power is *preserved through separation:* from our enemies, from the "other," from those we deem inferior to us.

A powerful but often neglected detail in the New Testament is the description of the curtain in the Temple being torn in half at the moment of Jesus's death. For centuries, the curtain *separated* the Holy of Holies from all other space in the Temple, and now that separation is metaphorically shredded. Behind what some scholars believe was a massive curtain blocking all light was the Ark of the Covenant, the symbol of not only God's dwelling place, but also of God's presence throughout Jewish history.[10] Is the tearing of this curtain a metaphor for a God no longer contained by time and space? Is God already and always present in every space, sacred or profane?

On that day when I baptized a dead baby, I never did answer all of the questions that tortured me. But even in this trauma, some clarity did come. Who is to say that the presence of God was not in the *act* of baptism itself, in the love and concern that brought us together, in the doctors' heroic efforts to save the child, in the tears of the nurses who could not? Because when everything is plunged into darkness, when our deepest hopes are dashed, when a baby dies in the womb, our first thought is often a universal cry of agony: *God help us.*

Perhaps it is not a favor we should be asking for, since it implies that a God who intervenes directly in human affairs could have prevented all this sadness. Perhaps our whole approach to religion needs to change—especially the way we pray. What has become clear to me after a lifetime in the ministry is that clarity comes in the *doing* of something good, and no clarity whatsoever comes in the *consideration* of the doing of something good. Religious institutions spend a lot of time and energy thinking about what people *should* do, and they are very good at recommending it. The problem comes when it is obvious that the life of faith is often subversive to the status quo. What happens when the message is taken seriously and becomes profoundly countercultural? This is when the church's house gets divided.

In the South, we have a saying for this: "He quit preaching and went to 'meddlin'!" Granted, the founder of our faith was executed for threatening the Roman Empire, so one might expect at least some discomfort in the sanctuary. But if your primary goal is institutional self-preservation, then you will always get nervous about people being offended, especially if they are big contributors. You will begin to imagine the loss of your church's reputation as a lovely, pleasant place to worship if people insist on welcoming "every single other." Radical hospitality sounds beautiful in theory. In practice it can open the church door to some very strange people, some of whom lack basic social graces, not to mention good grooming habits.

Alas, the church has lived more in fearful reticence than it has by the gospel mandate to "fear not." This has turned clergy into religious masters of ceremony on Sundays and customer-focused facilities managers during the week. Instead of lighting fires under people, they put them out. Instead of taking chances for justice, we try to calculate acceptable levels of risk should the church actually read and study its own scripture and then declare itself part of the Sanctuary Movement, for example.

This is crucial, because Jesus never says, "Go and *believe* likewise." The measure of an authentic spiritual life is in the way a follower *acts* in the world. Our real responsibility is summarized succinctly and beautifully by the prophet Micah. "He has told you, O mortal, what is good; and what does the

LORD require of you but to do justice, and to love kindness, and to walk humbly *with* your God?" (Micah 6:8, NRSV, emphasis mine).

Instead of bowing our heads and sending our prayers up and out on a journey to reach a remote deity, we should really pray *in all directions at once*. Instead of "worshipping" God (which assumes that for some reason God is the kind of being that wants and needs to be worshipped), we might draw near to the reality of God by revising the ancient cosmology of the heights and replacing it instead with a cosmology of the *depths*.[11] Our Beloved Communities could be "thin places" where heaven and earth meet, and where friends in the spirit seek access to the mystery, rather than entertaining bargains or offering bribes.

Perhaps the time has come for all of us who still have anything to do with organized religion (as well as those who describe themselves as "spiritual but not religious") to move away from a theology of obedience and embrace instead a *theology of consequence*. This is not meant to be just a clever turn of phrase. It represents a theological shift of the first magnitude. I grew up singing "Blessed Assurance," but what the world needs now is a "blessed assignment." Churches that will prosper in the future will be "doers of the word, and not merely hearers who deceive themselves" (James 1:22, NRSV).

Since the Enlightenment, we have all labored under a deadly illusion that reason will save us, or that there is something redemptive about our endless (and often incomprehensible) arguments about the existence or nonexistence of God, the metaphysics of the divinity of Jesus, or the latest guest list for the rapture. Danish philosopher Søren Kierkegaard knew that *concept* is not the same thing as *capacity*. One does not become gracious by reading a good book on grace. Knowledge is important, but *knowledge is not redemptive.*

I have sat in hospital rooms beside parishioners who have smoked two packs a day since they were teenagers. They often ask, "Why has God done this to me?" But if I plead with them before the diagnosis to stop smoking, reminding them that lung cancer is smoking's punishment, not God's, this is what they always say: "I know."

When I have counseled those who are addicted to drugs and alcohol, reminding them of the risks they are taking, I always ask simple questions. "Do you know where this is taking you? Do you know how badly this can end?" The answer is always the same: "I know."

When I sit with someone who has confessed to committing adultery, and who has no plans to stop, I will ask the person to consider what he or she stands to lose. "This could mean the end of your career, your place in the community, not to mention any future with your kids." And this is what I always hear: "I know."

Clearly, knowledge is not enough. The same can be said for what we call the "knowledge of salvation." The same can be said of what we have been told that we can "know" about God as both a lawgiver and judge. It is all unraveling, which is exactly what happens right before something new happens.

Not long ago I was speaking with a friend who attends a more conservative church in the suburb of Edmond, Oklahoma. This church, like the United Methodists, has decided not to welcome openly LGBTQ members and not to ordain gay clergy. It has also forbidden same-sex weddings on church property. It does this based on what the Bible "says" about homosexuality (all seven verses), based on the standard temple teaching that homosexual *activity* was idolatrous, non-procreative, and "against nature." But we are not first-century Jews. We understand today that no one knew anything at the time about sexual *orientation* or the possibility that same-sex couples could form lasting monogamous relationships with as much integrity as heterosexual couples (and sometimes with more).

When the subject of Mayflower Church came up in the conversation, my friend said something that goes to the heart of a theology of consequence. He said that he had been leading a Sunday-school class and discussing our decision to be an Open and Affirming congregation (United Church of Christ parlance for welcoming LGBTQ neighbors into the full sacramental hospitality of the church), when a woman said this: "Oh, Mayflower, of course. Those people are out there, and I don't agree with them on many things. But that church has a big heart."

I looked at my friend and said, "That's the best compliment we could ever receive." Knowledge is not redemptive, but love is.

After a lifetime of doing church, one thing has become abundantly clear to me. When it comes to finding our way in this divided world, we will not have much to offer if all we do is argue. Churches have been full of arguments, some of them noisy, bitter, and even deadly, since day one. Winning or losing them hardly matters to people looking for moral *behavior* and not just moral *clarity*. Or to help make this clear, just imagine that the life of Jesus had been a protracted debate, and that all we knew about him was that he won—that he was right.

By no means does our own desire to win—to be right—afflict only one party or persuasion. I have seen it on the left and on the right. Which is why our conception of God is so fundamentally important. If God is a lawgiver and judge, then we are trapped in an obsession with divine verdicts, instead of trusting in the consequences of our own divinely inspired actions. To be faithful means to live in an infinitely *entangled* universe. This is the lesson of quantum physics, which has now displaced Newtonian physics while the church was busy arguing over doctrine. It is time we awakened to this new reality, or got "woke," as the saying goes.

What if God is not trying to "save" us at all, but instead serves as a kind of cosmic blueprint for a moral order that is utterly, though incomprehensibly, dependable? What if we are called not to worship or fear any deity but to become mindful of both our choices and the infinite power of their consequences? God would no longer be the cosmic decider, or any sort of being at all. God would indeed be what Barbara Brown Taylor has called the Luminous Web—an unbroken promise that love multiplies love and hate multiplies hate because *there is no separation*. It all gives new meaning to an old maxim attributed to St. Augustine: *Without us God will not. Without God we cannot.*

2

Quantum Physics
and the Common Good

There is a living hum that might be coming from
my neurons but might just as well be coming from the
furnace of the stars. When I look up at them there is a small
commotion in my bones, as the ashes of dead stars that
house my marrow rise up like metal filings toward
the magnet of their living kin.

—Barbara Brown Taylor

Lamar Ashley lives with his wife, Abbie, on a small family
farm near Hennessey, Oklahoma. They are the modern
version of *American Gothic*. Their tools are high-tech—
farming apps and scientific instruments for testing their soil—
but their fingernails are still full of dirt. Some things never
change. From sunup to sundown, Abbie and Lamar do the
hardest work there is these days. They live on the land, with
the land, and off the land.

Abbie has been my wife's dear friend for over forty years.
They met when I was in seminary at Phillips University in
Enid, Oklahoma. They were both art students, and I was a

Jesus freak. Abbie taught us to love good barbecue, do the two-step, and buy a freezer big enough to hold a side of beef. Life was simple, and life was good. "Be good to the land," said Abbie, "and the land will be good to you."

What most people don't know, however, is that the community where Abbie and Lamar live is the earthquake capital of the world. In the last ten years, there have been more earthquakes in north-central Oklahoma than any other place on the planet—more than nine hundred in 2015 alone. And if you think the world's earthquake capital has to be California, Abbie and Lamar will sit you down at their dinner table with some unsweetened iced tea and tell you exactly why the ground is always shaking right outside their door. So often, in fact, that these days they just look at each other every time it happens. Awakened from sleep in the middle of the night, Abbie often asks, "Is that the trucks shaking the ground, or is that the ground shaking the trucks?" They say the cows get loud when the pastures move beneath them.

Not long ago, Oklahoma had so few earthquakes, and such small ones, that you would swear we never had them at all. All that changed, however, when the oil and gas industry, which dominates the state economy, began extracting its bounty in a new way. Until very recently, oil and gas wells were drilled vertically, or straight down. If you hit a pocket of oil or gas, you might strike it rich, but you could also come up empty—the dreaded "dry hole."

Exploration was slowing until the 1990s; many older but once-productive fields were considered past their prime and too expensive to drill. Then, as if a "savior" had appeared on the scene, a new way to extract oil and gas was born, based on two technologies. One was horizontal drilling, and the other was hydraulic fracturing, better known by its slang descriptor, "fracking."

Horizontal drilling was actually invented in a dentist's office in 1891, but not until 1929 was it applied to an oil well in Texas. By the 1980s, the process had improved, borrowing from the work of Thomas Leonard Watson, who used hydraulic fracturing to separate granite from bedrock in order to study granites. His low-water process was put on steroids. Now "millions of gallons of water, sand, and chemicals are pushed deep into the earth under high pressure to release small pockets of gas held tightly in the rock."[1] Oil and gas could now be captured from nonporous rock, such as shale.

In the fracking gold rush that followed, Oklahoma City was transformed by instant wealth. We have an NBA team (the Thunder), a new downtown skyline (with the gleaming Devon Tower), and a political ethos dominated by the empire that is oil and gas (no one fights it and wins). We also have a slow-motion environmental disaster on our hands. Earthquakes, exploding rigs, unregulated methane gas discharges, and polluted ground water for starters.

Abbie and Lamar are not tree huggers, but they will tell you matter-of-factly that the ground under their feet won't stop shaking until so-called injection wells are reduced, and the ocean of chemically laced wastewater (called "slickwater") being injected deep into the ground (because this is cheaper than "repurposing" it, as is required in other states) has altered the subterranean world in ways we never expected. Not only have we blasted rock formations once thought inaccessible to oil and gas extraction, but we may also be "lubricating" ancient fault lines that the oil and gas companies never bothered to map. Once those fault lines began to slip and the shaking started, it continued to spread out like an unstoppable ripple in an underground pond.

On the farm, healthy cattle have died after exposure to hydraulic fracturing fluid. Livestock are failing to reproduce, and stillborn and stunted calves have come after the mother was exposed to drilling wastewater. Dogs, cats, and horses have developed unexplained rashes and had difficulty breathing in areas of intensive drilling. "We are treating the earth like a sewer," Abbie said to me over dinner. "We are conducting an experiment on our own body, and what we hear is the groaning of our ancestors."

Abbie and Lamar both love to read Wendell Berry, but Lamar quotes from Gene Logsdon, one of the most influential agrarian writers in modern history. His book *Living at Nature's Pace* gets at the heart of the problem. Nature's way is the intended way for all creation, but instead of acting as stewards, keeping the garden and living at nature's pace, we live at the pace of business. "Our lives," writes Lamar, "easily devolve into a hopeless cycle of making and spending money . . . not around the earth's natural rhythms, sunrise and sunset, or rain and sunshine, winter and summer, but around the hours that we work to make money and then the hours in which the mall is open or the restaurant is open or the movie is showing."[2]

When Abbie and Lamar decided to build their "dream house," a one-room lean-to on the side of an old barn, they spent months living in a tent on the property. At night they watched the stars in near-total darkness; they studied the changing constellations; they made breakfast every morning at dawn and then worked the land until dusk, surviving 110-degree heat. They took joy at the end of each day when they literally *lay down on* the land. It was their pillow at night and their fierce dance partner by day. In the years since then, they have survived floods and droughts and the haunting howls of bobcats. But there was only one thing they could not survive.

They could not survive the greed of their fellow humans who decided to live *off* their land instead of living *on* it. The absentee landowners who moved to town and left their land to an invasion of speculators with fistfuls of cash. The fracking trucks that rumbled all night and tore up the roads. The thieves who stole the dark magic of the prairie by lighting up the landscape 24-7. The rigs, the drilling pads, the equipment that had to be lit all night so it would not be stolen—even the giant new wind farms, with their eerie vibrations, topped by red lights that strobe on and off in unison as far as the eye can see. Those surreal windmills popped up almost overnight, said Lamar, "like mushrooms after a spring rain." Rural life has been changed forever, he told me. The night is gone. The stars are gone. And the ground never stops shaking.

What does this have to do with God? As it turns out, everything—unless one thinks of God as somehow apart from the world, separate from creation, a distant observer of our high crimes and misdemeanors. Abbie and Lamar, and all the rest of us who live on a perishing planet, are witnessing the consequences of bad theology applied on a grand scale. That's because, without our realizing what was happening, a single word in the opening chapter of Genesis has been translated from the Hebrew with devastating effect:

> So God created humankind in his image, in the image of God he created them; male and female he created them. God blessed them, and God said to them, "Be fruitful and multiply, and fill the earth and subdue it; and have *dominion* over the fish of the sea and over the birds of the air and over every living thing that moves upon the earth" (Genesis 1:27–28, NRSV, emphasis mine).

The word is "dominion," and for centuries it has been interpreted to mean that humans have the right, even a responsibility, to rule the natural world—to "govern" the rest of creation. It establishes a hierarchy of power and authority, and the effect has been to regard the material world like a vast warehouse of resources for human exploitation. The hierarchy was set. God above humans, humans above animals, animals above all inanimate things—plants, trees, rocks. We would extend the hierarchy, of course, to male above female, white above nonwhite, European above non-European, straight above gay, and so forth. But "in the beginning," it was made perfectly clear that everything in creation knew its place and stayed in it. That is, until Copernicus and Galileo came along and displaced everything.

Now we live in a world in which the earth is no longer the center of the universe, and in which science has uncovered a new understanding of reality itself. For centuries, science and religion have been at odds with each other, because the church saw science as intent on putting God out of business. But in this chapter, we will explore why science not only is *not* the enemy of religion but may, in fact, now be its savior.

The Annoying Younger Brother

We can begin to make sense out of the way people talk about and understand God if we remember that our heads and our hearts have been divided since childhood. Not just politically and theologically, but also in the way that the SAT, that dreaded standardized test, divided us in school. We all got two completely separate scores—one verbal and one mathematical, as if these hemispheres of the brain were like the Hatfields and the McCoys. All of us were conditioned to believe that there are "verbal" people and there are "math" people, even though in reality there are poets who love calculus and botanists who love Rumi.

The relationship between science and religion has always been rocky, to put it mildly. When the Renaissance arrived, it was like an annoying younger brother had appeared on the scene to correct with dispassionate scientific logic everything that the church had explained in song and story. Before the Renaissance, there was only the firstborn son. His name was Tradition. He was obedient, he was orthodox, and he wore red shoes. He took the Bible seriously by taking it literally. Aristotle and Ptolemy had explained cosmology, and God was the reason for everything and the cause of everything.

The earth was the apple of God's eye. It sat exactly where God could keep a doting eye on it—right in the center of the universe. God's favorite creatures lived there, and stayed very busy having "dominion over the earth." Angels were said to push the planets around. Any questions?

Centuries after the Greeks figured out that the earth must be round—because, among other things, it cast a round shadow on the moon during a lunar eclipse—the church clung tenaciously to both a three-story, geocentric universe and a God in three persons. The trouble began almost immediately, however, since a God who is "up" and a hell that is "down" made a lot less sense on a round planet. As for the Trinity, "three in one and one in three" drove mathematicians (not to mention linguists) crazy and led to charges that Christians were polytheists who wanted to turn the Holy Spirit into an exclusive franchise for the Father and the Son. Before long, this burning question split the church into East and West: Is the Spirit the child of *both* the Father and the Son, or does it flow from the Father alone? At stake is whether the Spirit is an independent contractor, or whether the franchise belongs to Jesus. Constantinople said the Spirit is like a second child of the same Father. Rome said all three are unified by the same divine essence, which diminished the role of the Father in the eyes of Easterners.

Then, when Copernicus insisted that the earth circled the sun, and not the other way around, the church went into crisis mode. It condemned both Copernicus and Galileo for the sin of being right. Galileo had to get down on his knees and read a renunciation written for him by the church, and then spent the rest of his life under house arrest in a villa outside Florence. Because science and the Bible could not both be right, the older brother and the younger brother stopped speaking to each other. "Ever since then, science and religion have been engaged in a head-butting match. Science accuses religion of superstition and hyperbole; religion accuses science of nihilism and amorality."[3]

To be clear, the church already had a lot of blood on its hands. For centuries, Christians had killed nonbelievers in the name of Jesus, not to mention thousands of fellow Christians who went to war with one another over the precise meaning of the divinity of Jesus. Was he a man-bearing God, or a God-bearing man? Answer correctly, or you could be murdered by marauding bands of creedal fact-checkers. It is always sobering to remember that in the fifth and sixth centuries Christians killed more Christians over a single word in the creeds than so-called infidels in the Crusades and Inquisition.[4]

What ended this dark slumber was the same thing that fueled the Renaissance in the fifteenth century: the invention of the movable-type printing press. As Europe became more prosperous with the decline of famines and plagues, money was available to establish schools and colleges where the sons of gentlemen and nobles would receive a humanistic education imported from Italy. Johannes Gutenberg, a stonecutter and goldsmith, devised an alloy of lead, tin, and antimony that would melt at low temperatures and be durable in the press. Each letter could be used again and again to form words, sentences, and lines of text in infinite variety. The most important book to print was the Bible, of course, and Gutenberg tried to keep his technique a secret. He failed, and by the dawn of the sixteenth century, 2,500 European cities had acquired printing presses. The world would never be the same.

The printing press brought speed and standardized duplication to every work and provided a basis for scholarship by preventing further mistakes and alterations. As prices fell, more people than ever began to read, and to think for themselves, and to interpret the classics as well as the Bible. Libraries filled up with volumes that spread ideas quickly and with greater precision. Knowledge is power, indeed, and power began to shift from the clergy to the laity. Priests nervously drummed their fingers in secret meetings as more and more people showed up in church with their own Bibles. They had questions. They still do.

Meanwhile the annoying younger brother was the talk of the town. His first name was Science, his middle name was Logic, and his last name was Not-So-Fast. He was charismatic and iconoclastic, and the ladies loved him. He is the same guy who takes delight in telling you that Santa Claus does not exist and the Tooth Fairy is an early lesson in commodity-based capitalism. He explains myth as if it were an addiction of the weak-minded and the spirit as a stopgap fairy tale for everything that can't be explained by evidence-based reasoning. The strong do science. The weak do faith.

Little did the annoying younger brother know that he was trafficking in an illusion of his own—namely, that science deals exclusively with the observable, material world, while religion deals only with the invisible and nonmaterial. Or that science deals only with objective facts and unanimous opinion, while religion speculates about subjective relationships, ethics, and values. Both brothers were engaging in the kind of lazy thinking that always turns complicated ideas into false dichotomies.

When I teach critical thinking at the university, one of my favorite words to share with my students is the Greek word for any assumed major premise in a syllogistic argument: *enthymeme*. In the familiar deductive argument "All men are mortal; Socrates is a man; therefore Socrates is mortal," nobody really needs to state the major premise ("All men are mortal") because it is *assumed* to be true. It is an enthymeme.

I ask my students to consider whether or not we still make arguments using our own version of enthymemes. Can they name some? The hands go up, and we write modern enthymemes on the board: Wealth trickles down. More guns make us safer. Knowledge is redemptive.

Turns out, the definition of insanity—doing the same things over and over again and expecting different results—has its roots in assumed premises that may not be true. Socrates just as well could have said, "The unexamined *premise* is not worth living *by*." One thing that should be taught to every seminary student who plans to preach is that assumed premises are a form of mental laziness. It is driven by a desire to arrive at a *conclusion*, which in turn is also assumed. That is, until someone dares to stand up and say the emperor is naked.

Given that those of us in the church are ordained to preach in the name of a radical who upended the very definition of what it means to be faithful, a free pulpit may be one of the only places left where assumed premises can be challenged. Preaching is dangerous of course, and should be. We humans like our enthymemes. They are like our favorite pillow. Rather than change it out, we just flip it to the cool side and lie down again.

Each one of us retains something of the DNA from both the older and the younger brother. We long for the certainty of tradition, an infallible Bible, and the invisible moral authority of a sky God who has given us the Ten Commandments, not the Ten Suggestions. Life can be so hard, and sometimes it feels as if only the older brother can get us through it. But we are also the younger brother's kin—curious, open to new ideas, not fearful that science will destroy faith but hopeful that it might even deepen it. This sibling rivalry can appear every time we look through a telescope. The older brother in us will see a cosmic threat to the centrality of God's chosen ones on the pale blue dot, while the younger brother will be filled with awe and wonder, the true roots of religion. The former will double down on the need to secure our salvation, while the latter will choose to speculate on who else might be out there.

Meanwhile, back on earth the situation can get complicated, even schizophrenic. Pity the poor soul who has a PhD in evolutionary biology but is also a Southern Baptist. His church family will reject him for believing in evolution, and his scientific community will reject him for believing in God. Unless, of course, someone challenges the biggest enthymeme of them all: that they are not separate realms to begin with, just separate methods in search of the same unified mystery.

Goose Bumps in the Lab

When Stephen Hawking died, the world remembered him not only for his refusal to let Lou Gehrig's disease stop his mind from roaming the universe, but also for his obsession with what he called a "theory of everything." Instead of circling the theoretical wagons and confining himself to a single specialty, Hawking searched for a theory that would tie all theories together. He then talked about it using words that might make some scientists uncomfortable:

> If we do discover a complete theory, it should in time be understandable in broad principle by everyone, not just a few scientists. Then we shall all, philosophers, scientists, and just ordinary people, be able to take part in the discussion of why it is that we and the universe exist. If we find the answer to that, it would be the ultimate triumph of human reason—for then we would truly know the mind of God.[5]

The mind of *God*? Why did Hawking not say the mind of Science? Perhaps because, although he was by any conventional definition an atheist, he understood better than anyone that science and religion are both born of the same experience: awe and wonder. Ironically, Hawking was his own model of simultaneous entropy and expansion. His body was wasting away while his mind was set free to fill infinite space, including black holes. Like most scientists today, he favored the big bang as the most likely explanation for the origin of the universe.

As someone who leads a religious community, I wonder: What would a creation narrative sound like today if it were modeled on the big bang? Would it preach? Episcopal priest Barbara Brown Taylor once gave it a try, and it's worth reading:

> *Once upon a time, say fifteen billion years plus one day ago, neither "time" nor "space" had any meaning. There is not much more to say about that, except that nothing existed save a pinpoint of probability smaller than a proton that was the egg of the universe—which scientists call a "singularity." Then the egg exploded—who knows why— and the universe expanded a trillion trillion times, curving to such a degree that particles popped out of quantum nowhere. When the universe was one second old, "every spoonful of stuff was denser than stone and hotter than the center of the sun."*
>
> *   [. . .]*
>
> *All of this occurred in the first five minutes. After that, the universe settled into a half-million-year cooling cycle during which little else happened. The cosmos existed as a hot cloud of ionized hydrogen and helium. Then the temperature dropped some more and stars began to form under the influence of gravity. As they grew in mass, things heated up inside of them, turning them into nature's own nuclear fusion reactors. Using hydrogen as fuel, they converted the lighter elements into heavier ones such as carbon and iron. Eventually the new stars became middle-aged stars and finally old stars whose nuclear reactors broke down. Unable to defend themselves against their own gravity, the*

stars collapsed in on themselves, creating so much heat inside of them that they exploded in supernova. These were spectacular funerals. A supernova can release more energy in one minute than all the other stars in the sky combined. As is does, it bequeaths all its elements to the galaxy, seeding the cosmos with oxygen, carbon, hydrogen, and nitrogen.

If you remember your organic chemistry, then you know that these are the four elements most necessary for life. Our bodies are 65 percent oxygen, 18 percent carbon, 10 percent hydrogen, and 3.3 percent nitrogen, plus a smattering of the elements you can find listed on the bottle on your multi-mineral pills. Where did all those elements come from? From the creation of the cosmos. From the ashes of stars. Chemically speaking, the only difference between us and trees or rocks or chickens is the way in which our elements are arranged. During World War I, when blood was in short supply, wounded soldiers were sometimes transfused with seawater—and it worked! We are all made out of the same stuff. We are all children of the universe.[6]

Granted, this version of the story is a bit more complicated than "In the beginning when God created the heavens and the earth, the earth was a formless void and darkness covered the face of the deep, while a wind from God swept over the face of the waters" (Genesis 1:1–3, NRSV). But what is striking is not how different but how *similar* is the Hebrew poet's account of the same essential movement. From nothing to something. From darkness to light. From waters beneath to sky above. From the appearance of dry land to vegetation that carried its own future in its bosom (seeds). From a sun to rule the day to a moon to rule the night. From sterile sameness to shifting seasons that mark the passage of time. From dry riverbeds to savannas teaming with life. From silent skies to the sacred sound of Canadian geese flying overhead. From single-cell amoebas to sea monsters.

Finally, after the earth is crawling with living things, a fully self-conscious creature was made in God's image and given dominion over a planet that it would one day have the power to destroy. Even though we are often a sad and disappointing species, this is the most miraculous achievement of all. A creature that is capable of asking where it came from, where it is going, and to what, if anything, it belongs? Not even science has a clue where consciousness came from, or even what it is.

What is strikingly different about these two stories is that science emphasizes *unity* as cosmic evolution, albeit random, and Genesis emphasizes "separation"—a word used no less than five times in the first eighteen verses of the Bible (light from darkness, water from sky, day from night, sun from moon, and finally, humans from all other living things). It is almost as if the Hebrew poet was hoping to bring order out of chaos by establishing a cosmic hierarchy—where everything knows its place and stays in it. Perhaps he believed that his particular tribe could survive only if it remained pure, separate, and segregated—like the cosmos. Like every other tribe, the Judeans were taught to know who they were by knowing who, and what, they were not.

What matters now, especially on this shrinking planet, is

that we stop pretending that separation is what governs the physical (and spiritual) world. What we have learned from quantum physics, for example, is that reality itself refuses to be compartmentalized. This may sound unrelated to our views on God. But just as fracking brought instant wealth, it also brought other serious, even deadly environmental consequences. And this has everything to do with how we've partitioned the physical world from the spiritual one, pretending that God has bequeathed a cosmic inventory of natural resources to his chosen creatures as a gift, with no strings attached. As it turns out, *all the strings are attached.*

This is why more ministers need to read the Science section of *The New York Times*. We have left the impression, in countless sermons, that rocks are inert and animals are dumb, while people are animated and smart. What's more, says the church, we people are wretched and lowly sinners by birth, while God is some invisible heavenly perfection. Up and down the line, separation is the order of the universe, unless you are a quantum physicist who is baffled by the way subatomic particles behave. Strange things have been happening in the lab for a long time, and it should matter to you even if you don't know a thing about quarks, fractals, or nonlinear equations.

In particular, something called quantum entanglement might need to become required reading in seminary. Based on the baffling reality that subatomic particles that decay into two particles become a set of twins—a single system with two parts, spinning in opposite directions—Einstein and two of his colleagues at Princeton, Boris Podolsky and Nathan Rosen, tried, in a famous experiment, to disprove the theory that if the spin of one of the "twins" is reversed, the spin of the other will also reverse, no matter how far apart the particles travel. This suggested that there is some kind of instantaneous superluminal communication between quantum particles that exceeds the speed of light. This bothered Einstein no end because it violated his theory of special relativity and gave scientific support to what would later be called "field theory." In what has been called the single most important discovery in all of physics, normally reserved scientists confessed that there is "no known mechanism" for this phenomenon and suggested that our previous understanding of time and space might be incorrect—or to put it theologically, made in the image of humans. The separation that we perceive in the universe may in fact be an illusion at the subatomic level. Einstein called it "spooky action at a distance."[7]

Collective Responsibility

When Sir Isaac Newton established the laws of celestial dynamics, he described a solar system that acted like a vast machine. It was made up of separate parts, some as small as the atom, some as large as the sun, but they all worked together in predictable ways. All big things could be broken down into small things.

Not surprisingly, humans began to model their worldview and institutions after the prevailing physics of the day. When this model is transposed to the human universe, the individual being becomes the atom—the single unit of social matter that is the basic building block for all social groupings. Nations, communities, churches, and families are all reducible to the individuals who make them up. If a child acts out, take the child to a counselor. Fix the child without ever inquiring into the health of the family. "If a poor woman sells crack to feed her children, send the woman to jail. Punish the woman, without ever asking about the society in which she lives. . . . There is nothing wrong with the whole that cannot be fixed by tinkering with the parts. . . . The individual is the fundamental unity of reality."[8]

This illusion of separation works to shield us all from collective responsibility. After a Sunday-morning sermon on racism, one of my parishioners said to me matter-of-factly, "I never owned any slaves." At first I did not know how to respond, since neither of us was old enough to have been given the opportunity. But at a deeper level, I knew exactly what she meant. Evil is an individual phenomenon, she was saying, not a collective one. Even though the church itself carries the enduring stain of either supporting slavery (often by quoting Romans 13) or refusing to take sides, which was itself taking a side, the idea that one is absolved from injustice because one did not overtly participate in the injustice itself is a kind of Newtonian fiction. "I was not one of the broken parts," she was saying, "so I don't have to worry about the failure of the machine."

This is a comforting fiction, but also the source of the deep sickness of our time. But now, thanks to the offspring of the annoying younger brother, scientists have discovered what mystics have known all along: *The whole, not the parts, is the fundamental unit of reality.* Everything is connected to everything else. Individuals are not the reality of the quantum age.

Systems are. Solar systems. Family systems. Educational systems. Political systems. You name it. If the common good has
disappeared, it is not because there's an insufficient number
of uncommonly good people in the world. Rather, the problem is that not enough people do what is right without expecting their individual contributions to be noted. We are not
independent Newtonian contractors working toward individual outcomes. Every good deed, however large or small, gets
tossed into the Luminous Web. All we can do is trust (have
faith) that it will vibrate its way across the universe and help
to make the common good both more common and more
good.

God bless Albert Einstein, who was a baffling and redemptive combination of a human supercomputer and a tenderhearted innocent. It was Einstein who said, "The most
beautiful thing we can experience is the mysterious. It is the
source of all true art and science. He to whom this emotion is
a stranger, who can no longer pause to wonder and stand rapt
in awe, is as good as dead."

I once attended a preaching conference at Princeton, where
Einstein taught for many years, and happened to sit down on
a campus bench without realizing whose bench I was sitting
on. It had a plaque, of course, but I was too busy to read it. I
had a sermon to write, and so I was oblivious to my surround-
ings until my preaching professor, the renowned Fred Craddock, came strolling by.

"Robin, do you know where you are sitting?" he said. I
looked up, confused.

"You are sitting on the Einstein bench. He used to sit there
after staying up all night, his amazing mind screwed down on

top of an equation none of us could comprehend. Then, by the morning light, he would laugh at the sight of a child losing a race with a melting ice cream cone. Do you know where you are sitting, Robin? That better be a good sermon."

I laughed, as Craddock so often made people do, and then I pondered the deeper meaning behind his words. Sitting on the Einstein bench got me thinking about the enormous shift that seems to be occurring as we pass the five hundredth anniversary of the Protestant Reformation. What had been religion's nemesis for centuries—the annoying younger brother—has lately become the true architect of awe and wonder.

One can only wonder if perhaps the idea of the Field, the unbroken and deeply mysterious interconnectedness of physical matter across time and space, also has a *spiritual* dimension that the older brother could not have understood. Separation appears to be the essential lesson of faith traditions, reinforced by scriptural encouragement to overcome it or to be rescued from it. But if love can connect us as seamlessly as quantum particles can remain "twins" across intergalactic distances, then the apostle Paul's ode to the *end of separation* in Romans 8 has a new ring: "For I am convinced that neither death, nor life, nor angels, nor rulers, nor things present, nor things to come, nor powers, nor height, nor depth, nor anything else in all creation, will be able to separate us from the love of God in Christ Jesus our Lord" (Romans 8:38–39, NRSV).

Honesty requires us all to admit that if there was a big bang, none of us know what came before it, or who lit the match. What scientists do know, however, is that if there was a big bang, there should be evidence of cosmic radiation left over from the heat of the original explosion. When they started building special antennae to pick up this theoretical cosmic hiss, and they heard something, they first mistook it for a kind of irritating static. But it never stopped, and it came from all directions at once. Then they realized that it was indeed the cosmic radiation "echo" they had been searching for.[9] Now we know that creation left not just footprints but audio. The universe is still murmuring a song of itself, which gives a whole new twist to the old words of the apostle Paul that faith comes from what is heard (Romans 10:17).

If science can point us toward an undivided physical universe, then why can't religion point us toward an undivided ethical universe in which no action, no matter how small, is inconsequential? What if every move we make, especially our moral and ethical decisions, vibrates a strand of the Luminous Web, and the whole universe shivers? What if so-called unintended consequences reveal just how mindless we really are when it comes to moral cause and effect? Consequences are indeed indifferent to intentions, which is why they do not excuse actions that we refuse to think through carefully in the first place. If there is at the heart of creation a deep and dependable equilibrium, then God is as good a name for it as we can come up with. When we destroy ourselves with bad choices, on the other hand, the devil did *not* make us do it. We have just stopped paying attention and then gone in search of a scapegoat.

While Oklahoma preachers were praising the instant wealth created by our fracking boom, implying that God was rewarding us by transforming us into a "big-league city," they

conveniently avoided Psalm 24, which challenges the owner-
ship of mineral rights altogether: "The earth is the Lord's and
all that is in it" (Psalms 24:1, NRSV).

Oklahoma clergy routinely thank God in their prayers for
the miraculous technology that is fracking, when what they
are really thankful for is the wealth it has created. It would be
better to ask forgiveness for the consequences of something
God had nothing to do with. This is precisely the problem
with objectifying the divine and then placing it on retainer. It
removes the idea that the divine itself is being wounded in
the world and that we are to blame for what Matthew Fox
called "matricide."

It would be better if clergy would stop obsessing over what
people "believe" and ask instead that we all pay closer attention to each and every choice we make, regardless of inten-
tion, and then observe carefully what sort of real-world
consequences will follow *before* we die. If this sounds a lot like
Buddhism, so be it. I find nothing particularly offensive about
being referred to as a "Buddhist Christian" or even a "Christo-
centric Unitarian" (both of which are labels used to describe
me and my ministry). I am interested in wisdom as a way of
being in the world, not the incarnation as a singular metaphysical occurrence unavailable to the rest of us. An emphasis
on wisdom could actually unite the world's religions because
it is grounded in behavior, not belief.

In the West, the cult of the individual turns all of us into
selfish independent contractors. To change the world, however, one need not look for something grand or earthshaking
to do every day. Just think about someone other than yourself. Call a spouse or partner to explain why you will be late

or to ask what sounds good for dinner, or tell someone for no apparent reason that you love her, or him, even though it is not Valentine's Day. Remember, the patron saint of that commercial lovefest is a bi-diapered infant and blindfolded to boot! Wisdom can save us all—but only if we act on behalf of others. Wisdom acts as if it trusts deeply in an entangled and consequential world. This is not a doctrine. This is reality. You can experience it every day. You can *believe* it.

Humans are fond of calling things "coincidences." Often they are cited as proof that an invisible hand is pulling the strings. Stephen Hawking died on Einstein's birthday. Is that a coincidence? My grandmother used to say, "There are no coincidences. There are only times when God wishes to remain anonymous." If she had studied quantum theory, however, she might have said, "See how the Luminous Web occasionally gives us a rare glimpse of itself." But that would not sound like my grandmother.

As a pastor, I have long asked my congregants to just study their own lives more carefully. Put down your cell phone and look at the real world again. Look long, look hard, look carefully, and then use your heart as well as your eyes. The scientific and the spiritual will suddenly appear to be a vast conspiracy of infinitely entangled consequences. In the end, each one of us is a jumbled but revealing aggregate of the decisions we have made, both large and small. There is no opting out.

Granted, this idea of God as the Luminous Web may seem abstract and disembodied. But it actually calls for us to be more concrete and embodied. Religion in the West is profoundly overintellectualized, and we need to get faith out of the head and return it to the real habits of the heart. There is no risk, after all, in going to a lecture on quantum physics, asking a few good questions, and then going home to feel deliciously superior. It is just as easy to be enthralled by a TED talk on the empathic imagination and then pass by a homeless person outside the auditorium without even making eye contact. I can study chaos theory and then exempt myself from recycling, thinking that my two cents have nothing to do with that small continent of plastic debris floating in the Pacific. I can feel deliciously superior to those who do not understand Heisenberg's uncertainty principle (as if I really understood it myself), without so much as translating a word of it into an ethical imperative. At some point, however, one must take the longest trip that any of us will ever take—the journey between the head and the heart.

The God we need now should insult neither science nor the saints. Like leaven in the loaf, it can rise into the banquet of a new theology and new action. No more tinkering around the edges or rearranging the deck chairs on the *Titanic*. How *would* we live and work and pray in community together if God is not pulling the strings, but rather God *is* the string?

3

Sin as the Illusion That We Are Home Alone

It is by going down into the abyss that we recover the treasures of life. Where you stumble, there lies your treasure.

—JOSEPH CAMPBELL

Professor Midlife was restless. He had started telling his friends that his marriage seemed to be "losing its passion." Everyone knew this was shorthand for what he really meant—that he was dissatisfied with his sex life. His friends were left to guess whether this meant he wasn't having sex very often, or whether the sex he was having didn't compare to the porn he was watching. Meanwhile, no one was honest enough to admit that they weren't having sex like that either, since porn and sex have almost nothing to do with each other.

Still, those counterfeit images filled the gallery of his mind, and he confused them with reality. He became increasingly certain that by comparison with the world of sexual fantasy, he was trapped in the real world instead of the other way around. He shopped online for the most arousing scenes, but this produced diminishing returns. It left him conflicted about his own hang-ups, not to mention increasingly bored with the connection between real intimacy and real sex.

She was a graduate student. Dark hair. Full lips. Not to mention a compelling constellation of freckles. When Professor Midlife called her name, she always turned her head and smiled, then leaned forward and thrust out her chin as if to meet an imaginary kiss. He did not mean to go on thinking about her after class, but she reminded him of lines from an E. E. Cummings poem: "thy mouth is as / a chord of crimson music / Come hither / O thou, is life not a smile?"

As winter turned to spring, so did her clothing. Professor Midlife found himself gazing at her when she wasn't looking and convinced himself that she was doing the same. One day, as he watched her take an exam, he remembered yet more lines from the same poet: "thy breasts are swarms of white bees / upon the bough of thy body / thy body to me is April / in whose armpits is the approach of spring."

After class, he looked up the poem and read it aloud to himself. Why he did this was something of a mystery, even to him. Perhaps he thought this might make a dangerous situation seem normal. As if, when one teaches poetry and is falling in love with a student, it is better to drape the obsession in the subject matter. That way, you feel as if you are simply standing in a long line of eloquent victims.

They met for the first time in her apartment off campus when her roommate was away. The sex was both awkward and frenzied, but the novelty of it overwhelmed the shame. Neither one of them dared to admit that in addition to getting the attention they both needed, it also felt like they were *falling*—falling into a place from which they could not extricate themselves. Ironically, Professor Midlife had even taught this lesson in class. "When bodies lie down together," he had said in a lecture once, "they make an unspoken promise that requires the breaking of so many other promises." She had nodded her pretty head in agreement.

Now began the real work, which was to keep from getting caught. Given the gravity of the consequences, it was important for Professor Midlife to maintain the appearance of virtue and good judgment while talking himself into believing that this was something he *deserved*, given how misunderstood he was at home. The student, for her part, wasn't sure how she felt. One day she felt powerful. The next day she felt pathetic. For the first time in her life, she thought about killing herself.

For the first time in his life, Professor Midlife wished there were still pay phones. Cell phones are like keeping a murder weapon in your pocket. They light up at the most inconvenient times, especially next to the bed where your wife is sleeping. A secret email account is required, of course, but even this is dangerous. We all know that every message tapped out by flying thumbs is forever. These are the electronic fossils of the age; when someone needs one, they can always dig it up. Not like love letters, easily burned in the fireplace. Now every message you mindlessly surrender to the overlords of the Internet is like a file that can never be deleted.

The summer turned to fall, and with the resumption of classes, she started dating someone new, someone her own age. Professor Midlife pretended not to care, of course, because he had no right to care. But in reality, he was devastated. He had no choice now but to admit that he was old and would never be young again. The sex had become perfunctory, devoid of eye contact, and followed by no conversation, just dressing and leaving. There was no electricity in her touch, no warmth in her fingers, no tenderness in her kisses. It was over. It just wasn't resolved.

Why is it, Professor Midlife wondered, *that it is so much harder to end relationships than it is to begin them?* He remembered a line from Graham Greene's *The End of the Affair:* "As long as one suffers one lives."

Each of them practiced their lines for leaving, but they never got the chance to deliver them. A large envelope arrived in the professor's mailbox at home one day. It was addressed to his wife, but not from *her.* As it turned out, it was from a female friend who had figured out what was happening and decided to let the wife know, as the opening line put it, "what your husband has been up to in his spare time."

Inside the envelope was a collection of emails written over the months between the professor and his student. They had been hacked, or so the informant claimed, from his secret email account. Needless to say, all hell broke loose.

It was not the kind of hell that preachers are so fond of describing, however. It was not about being punished after death. Rather, this was hell on earth, that very particular and toxic kind of hell that follows from the loss of *trust*—the sacred trust that holds the world together. Lying about little things is one thing. Lying about big things drops the floor out from underneath the very possibility of human happiness. Why?

Trust makes all things possible. It binds our lives, like the spine of a book. When trust is gone, the pages of life fall out and the story ends. Relationships make us happy, not things, and trust makes relationships possible. Which is just another way of saying that lying unravels the world. As that universal fable "The Boy Who Cried Wolf" makes clear, when one cannot be believed, one becomes in-credible. When one has no credibility, one disappears, even when one is telling the truth. To make matters worse, no one knows how to restore trust once it is lost. There is no known formula, no proven recipe, and no trendy therapy that can bring it back. Trust is the earth-bound version of faith, but trust is not an infinitely renewable resource. A person who can't be believed is a person who can't be loved.

Over the months that followed, as the professor and his wife struggled to save their marriage, one truth emerged that seemed particularly obvious. *His wife had known all along that something was going on.* The changes had been small but obvious. He was always running nondescript "errands." He took showers and did his laundry in the middle of the day, lest *her* scent linger. He changed his personal grooming habits, claiming that he had just discovered the benefits of waxing. Then she found a toothbrush in the glove compartment of his car.

Even on those occasions when he brought gifts to her, or seemed unusually solicitous and attentive, she intuited that he was compensating. At a deep but unmistakable level, she knew that he was lying. None of this, however, was as compelling as his incremental separation from her in bed. She knew he was thinking of someone else when they made love—that, although he looked right at her, he was also looking right through her. Intimacy, as it turns out, cannot be feigned. Lovers become quantum twins, and nothing can hap-

pen to one that does not affect the other. Call it "spooky action at a distance."

So why had she not confronted him about it sooner? Well,
what would he have said? Besides, she did not want it to be
true either. Deception is a kind of co-conspiracy for those
who prefer it. As the evidence of the affair accumulated,
however, it also pointed to a larger truth. Namely, that *both
material and spiritual separation are ultimately impossible*. As
with our abuse of the physical world and the lies we tell to
cover it up, so, too, are human beings prone to abuse their
spiritual covenants and then lie to cover it up. We can delude
ourselves into thinking that we are the exception to the Luminous Web, that we are entitled to pretend that what we do
alone in our rooms will not infect the whole house. But this,
too, is a lie. We vibrate no single strand of the web in isolation.
We manufacture the illusion of separation at our own peril.

Professor Midlife was well aware of Sir Walter Scott's famous line about the dangers of deception: "Oh what a tangled
web we weave, / when first we practice to deceive!" It comes
from his romance *Marmion* and refers to a love triangle that
doesn't end well. But it is one thing to teach the poem and
quite another to be trapped inside it. Today we might alter
the saying slightly in light of quantum physics. "Oh how we
tangle the web *itself* when first we practice to deceive."

In the Hebrew scriptures, there is a line that baffled me
when I first ran across it in seminary. In Leviticus, the author
offers this strange admonition: "Do not curse the deaf or put
a stumbling block in front of the blind, but fear your God. I
am the LORD" (Leviticus 19:14, New International Version).

I remember thinking to myself, *OK, a stumbling block—*

that makes sense, because a blind person might actually stumble over it. But never curse a deaf man? Why not? He can't hear you. Maybe you are having a bad day and need to toss out a few expletives. Why not turn them loose on a deaf man? No harm, no foul, right?

Like any good graduate student, I asked my professor for help. His answer is one I will never forget. "Robin," he said, "it's true that the deaf man would not hear you. But *you* would hear you. And the rabbis believed that *God* would hear you. And two out of three is not bad."

As I thought about this for a moment, the professor continued. "Think about all those people who don't go to see their loved ones who are living with dementia. They say, 'She wouldn't even know that I was there.' That might be true, but *you* would know that you were there, and *God* would know that you were there, and again, two out of three is not bad."

Unoriginal Sin

The great Presbyterian minister Ernest Campbell joked to me once, "Robin, ministers of the gospel are in favor of the *reduction* of sin, but we do not favor its complete elimination. Otherwise, we would be unemployed!"

Fair enough, but let's be honest. The church has used the word "sin" like a hammer. Although the first of the seven deadly sins is pride, not lust, the church has an undeniable obsession with "perversions" of the flesh. What about the daily perversions in the boardroom, in the courthouse, on Wall Street, or in those gilded chambers where secret handshakes and backroom deals oppress the poor? Why does so much preaching make God out to be a voyeur who is more interested in sex than in greed? For the answer, we need only look in the mirror.

This imbalance has led many progressive Christians to reject the use of the word "sin" altogether. That's unfortunate, because when used to describe our toxic selfishness, our entitled apathy, our world-destroying illusions of separation, "sin" is exactly the right word. It goes straight to the heart like an arrow. It delivers a demand that we repent, which is another word we don't like, even though it only means to "turn around." We don't like the word "confession" either, since it presumes that we have fallen short and need to be honest about it. Well, good luck disproving that.

Still, Christian ministers like me haven't helped much with this situation. When asked to define sin, the evangelist Billy Graham put it this way: "A sin is any thought or action that falls short of God's will. God is perfect, and anything we do that falls short of His perfection is sin." His *perfection*? One can only wonder how much harm this definition of sin has done in the world. How much guilt has it generated? How much power has it given evangelists to define and then demand the only means to forgiveness and salvation? Sin is falling short of perfection? This is an impossible bargain, to imagine a perfect God and then to insist that this source of all perfection is keeping a perfect but perpetually disappointed eye on you at all times. No wonder people say religion has been responsible for both the best things in the world and the worst.

Take original sin. It was mostly Augustine's invention, this idea that we are born bad, that we arrive in the world as little sinners, bearing the sinful DNA of that mythical couple, Adam and Eve. Even though original sin is nowhere to be found in the Hebrew or Christian scriptures, the church created this doctrine as the fundamental premise of orthodoxy—the granddaddy of all religious enthymemes. It posits that we are trapped, that we are helpless, that sin is our destiny and therefore we can't save ourselves—that is, until we confess Jesus as Lord and Savior. This does not remove sin from us, of course, but we are now forgiven.

It seems like an oddly futile enterprise to forgive humans for what they can't help doing and will continue doing. Until you consider how it gives the church enormous power. The doctrine of original sin created the *ultimate spiritual franchise*, diagnosing the human race with a disease that only the church could cure.

Not long ago, I was driving past a church in Oklahoma where the sermon titles are posted on a sign near the street. It said in big block letters: IF YOU ARE DONE WITH SIN, THEN COME ON IN. When I got closer, however, I saw that someone had written another message underneath it. The letters were smaller and looked like lipstick. *But if you're not quite through, call 272 . . .*

This is how religion becomes a cartoon. Until we stop thinking about sin as an individual transgression against a cosmic calculator of individual offenses, we will remain helpless and in need of rescue. Our sins are not against God but against our neighbor, in whom the spirit of God resides. Or as a cowboy poet put it once, "Most human misery is caused by miserable human beings."

Even so, no physician would treat only the symptom of a disease. First she would uncover the root cause. Until one's separation is restored—from oneself as well as from the neighbor—the damage will be never-ending. We are not sinning because we can't help ourselves. Rather, we do harm to the neighbor because we live under the most dangerous of all illusions: that we are exempt from the entanglements that bind us together with everything that is, or was, or ever will be. Sin is not an inheritance. It is the bastard child of entitled thinking. It is conceived in the delusion that we are home alone. It is the child of self-deception. Sin is not a "bad seed" but an existential selfishness. *I am immune,* says every lost and dangerous human being, *from the consequences that bind other human beings.*

As long as sin is understood as an individual infraction against the laws of God, rather than the effects our actions have on our neighbor, the world, even the universe—our religious rituals will reinforce a kind of theological privilege. Not unlike with white privilege, which is America's real original sin, we may look toward heaven with a wink and a prayer for forgiveness. But the real damage is done on earth, against those whose suffering will be passed on ad infinitum. Selfishness and cruelty are the gifts that keep on giving. Love multiplies into infinity as well. The choice is ours.

Some of our wisest voices have tried to move us away from a transactional view of sin and define it as relational, grounded, and consequential. When we act out of fear and selfishness, instead of faith, we sin. Hildegard of Bingen, a twelfth-century Christian mystic, said that sin is a "drying up." It is care-less-ness, and use-less-ness. It is a lack of passion, a kind of sterility in producing good fruit. Rosemary Radford Ruether, a contemporary feminist theologian, put it this way: "What is appropriately called sin belongs to a more specific sphere of human freedom where we have the possibility of enhancing life or stifling it."[1]

These definitions expand our understanding of sin to include more than just individual failures of the flesh, emphasizing that sin is also about the collective power of our *choices*. Fathers destroy their families not just by adultery but by physical and emotional absence—choosing another late night at the office, or a boys' night out, over attendance at a child's recital or birthday party. In a unified spiritual world, death comes also by a million small cuts. We are perpetually engaged in the act of making or unmaking the world.

Spiritual theologian Matthew Fox once compiled a list of the "Ten Deadly Sins" of our time.[2] He said that whenever we choose to add *suffering* to an already suffering world, that is sin. When we *ignore*, choose not to see, not to hear, or not to feel. When we choose to be *unbalanced*, overly committed to our tribe or worldview. When we *sever relationships*, cut ourselves off from others and from the universe. When we are guilty of *dualism*, seeing the world as either/or, segregating it around race or class or gender. When we are *reductionists*, oversimplifying the depth, intensity, or complexity of our relationships. When we *lose passion*, replacing curiosity and creativity with mind-numbing entertainment or soul-diminishing indulgences. When our *love is misdirected*, our energy is *dissipated*, or our choices *devour and destroy* everything that is good, beautiful, and true—this is sin.

Telescopic Philanthropy

In Charles Dickens's *Bleak House*, there is a character named Mrs. Jellyby. She is always having guests over for dinner to discuss her charitable work, all while ignoring the fate of her own children. When we first meet her, one of the little Jellybys has gotten his head caught between a couple of iron railings and is howling in distress. Inside the house, her other children wander the darkened rooms and one of them trips and falls down the stairs, his head bumping loudly on several landings as the invited guests wince in sympathetic pain. You can always recognize a Jellyby child by its bruised knees, runny nose, and empty stomach.

Mrs. Jellyby pays no attention to any of it. She is a plump, pretty woman between forty and fifty with very handsome eyes—although, as Dickens puts it, "they had a curious habit of seeming to look a long way off. As if . . . they could see nothing nearer than Africa." That's because her mission work is focused on helping people who live on another continent, a couple of thousand miles away, whom she has never met. On fire to save them, she invites waves of Victorian ladies over for tea and then washes it down with tales of distant despair and the need to take up a collection to rescue other people's children.

Dickens, in a marvelously snide phrase, calls this, "telescopic philanthropy"—that warmth of heart for people made exotic by distance, while all around, in one's own house, there are people who could use our help. Such fixation is the curse of well-meaning human beings everywhere—including you and me, if we're being honest. What's more, our religious training often intensifies this problem by creating a dependence on a God made exotic by distance.

In counseling sessions, countless grown children have told me how their very busy and self-important fathers never had time for them. "My father has written twenty books," one man said, "but I wish he had given me the time he took to write just one of them." A girl struggling with drugs and alcohol, not to mention serial failed relationships, confessed to me that her dad had been the most prominent person in her community but spent most of his time looking right over the top of her head. Yet another woman said that her father never picked out a thoughtful gift for her at Christmas—he just wrote checks that he tucked into her stocking. When she confessed to being unhappy at home, he responded by putting in a swimming pool.

Even the great Russian novelist Leo Tolstoy, a man who wrote eloquently about living the way of love, struggled to do so with those around him. He claimed to be the only person who understood the true message of Jesus but was compulsively unfaithful to his wife and largely absent from his children. Only a year into a marriage so oppressive that Sophia often considered suicide, she wrote in her diary about the chasm between her husband's idealism and his behavior. "If he had one iota of the psychological understanding which fills his books, he would have understood the pain and despair I was going through." How ironic that at the same time Tolstoy told the story of an aristocratic woman at the theater weeping at imaginary tragedy enacted on the stage, while outside in the cold, "her old and faithful coachman, awaiting her in the bitter winter night, is freezing to death."[3]

Over my lifetime as a pastor, it has surprised me to learn how often human beings can wall off one part of themselves from another. We have our eyes cast far off, and we prefer ethereal abstractions to concrete realities. An appropriate prayer in church these days would be simple and optical in nature: "Holy one, make us nearsighted."

A friend and colleague, Dr. Tom Boyd, once used a memorable analogy to describe this phenomenon of primal separation. When his first son was only about two or three weeks old, he and his wife would place the baby in the middle of the bed, on his back. Boyd noticed that, periodically, as the newborn's arms and legs flailed, "he suddenly jerked, and a momentary fear seemed to register on his face. This kept happening to him," he recalled, "and it bothered me. He was the first kid, and I wanted everything to be perfect. I worried that he might be spastic."

When Boyd and his wife visited the pediatrician, they asked her about these jerks, this sudden "clenching" of the air.

"Oh, he's jerking because he can't find the edge," she said.

"Edge? Edge of what?"

"The womb," she responded. "He's been closely confined there for nine months, and he's seeking some limit, because he can't really imagine where he is without it."

The pediatrician suggested swaddling their son or putting pillows on each side of him—a prescription familiar to anyone who has ever had children or observed a baby in the crib. They all "clench" at the air, as if trying to draw this new strange, unbounded space back around them; to exist in a manageable space again.

It must have felt this way to all of us, even if we can't remember it. Our first feeling was in fact the panic of having "fallen" into a strange and frightening new universe without limits. Our existential response is to "clench" at the air in myriad ways, to get things under control again. Over a lifetime, we shadowbox this boundlessness, frantically and often destructively, in order to make the angst of the free fall of finitude go away. Just ask Professor Midlife.

The philosopher Martin Heidegger had a term for our finite encounter with infinity. He called it "throwness." Dr. Boyd elaborates:

> *We're cast into the abyss of human existence, and we must find our way within the conditions available. This is our foundational double bind. We are terrified by the lack of edges, the threat to our finite condition, but we're at the same time fascinated and drawn beyond the edge. We suffer the urge to enter infinite possibility and at the same time to confine it and bind it to the limitations of our own finitude. We lust for infinity, but we become lost in the details of our finitude. This is the thrall and thrill of existence.*[4]

This "throwness" as primal separation can also manifest itself in deadly ways. Charles Manson grew up the son of a teenage prostitute. As a child, little Charlie fell asleep every night to the sounds of his mother entertaining her clients in the next room. When he created a cult called the Manson Family, was he replacing the one he never had? In this netherworld of psychedelic drugs and adoring (or brainwashed) female subordinates, Manson's rage morphed into religious

delusions. He thought he was the Messiah and had a fascination with Armageddon, the Beatles' song "Helter Skelter," and
what he prophesied was a coming race war and nuclear apoc-
alypse.

When his murderous campaign ended in the brutal slay-
ings of actress Sharon Tate and other Hollywood residents,
the world was shocked by details of the crime—especially the
stabbing death of Tate, who was eight months pregnant, by
Manson Family member Susan Atkins. She refused Tate's
pleas for mercy and then used Tate's blood to write the word
"pig" on the front door.

If ever the world could be justified in naming a clear man-
ifestation of pure evil, this was the moment. Preachers took
to their pulpits eager to prove that Satan is real and that Manson was the Antichrist. What was not talked about, however—
what was lost in our fascination with the unspeakable—were
the words that psychologists used to describe Manson's murderous pathology. It was marked by "rejection, instability, and
psychic trauma" and "constantly striving for status and to secure some kind of love." Or, to put it another way, by a life
spent trying to kill his mother.

Ideally, the religious impulse is born of this desire to overcome such primal separation. After all, the word "religion"
comes from the Latin word *ligare*, meaning to join or link,
reuniting the human and divine. But as religious systems
evolve from revelation to regulation, they seek power over
their followers. In the end, they do more "clenching" than
binding, offering not a new way of being in the world but, as
Kierkegaard put it, a way "to secure ourselves against our own
insecurity." We clench at infinity by denying it, or by substi-

tuting more manageable forms of pseudo-infinity, or by employing what Dr. Boyd calls the most common strategy of all: We *distract* ourselves through compulsive preoccupation with what we believe to be of ultimate concern.[5]

I have often experienced this tension between what Heidegger calls "throwness" in my relationships with estranged parishioners. Once, years ago, an elderly woman in my congregation was upset that I did not seem to be as fond of the "old-time gospel hymns" as she was. In particular, we had not sung "Battle Hymn of the Republic" in worship for what seemed to her to be an unacceptable, even scandalous, length of time. To be clear, she'd been suspicious about my patriotism, as well as my theology, ever since I preached that sermon about how military images in hymns were a contradiction of the gospel.

In essence, she had grown more and more anxious about, even terrified by, the "lack of edges," as Heidegger would say, and needed to clench at something to save her church. One day she issued a simple ultimatum. "Robin, we will sing 'Battle Hymn of the Republic' in the next six weeks or I will leave the church."

Clergy call this the blackmail model of worship planning. Congregants who were there before the minister arrived, and will be there after he is gone, maintain their power over "their church" by raising the stakes for the minister. *Let us test this young whippersnapper, and if he fails, I will take my good taste in hymns and my money someplace else.* Meanwhile, there is no pastor alive who does not recognize that responding to threats is a leadership black hole from which there is no escape.

Needless to say, we did not sing "Battle Hymn of the Republic" during the six-week trial period, and she did indeed leave the church. We limped along for several years without her support, and then word reached me one day that she was in the ICU, gravely ill, dying from congestive heart failure.

So what was I supposed to do, refuse to visit her? I had those pesky ordination vows to follow, the ones that insist that I see Christ in everyone I meet. Really? Everyone?

Even so, I felt anxious. The visit itself was fraught with my own "lack of edges." *What if this visit does nothing to help her? What if she dies upon my entering the room? What if she waves me off and tells the nurses not to allow me back in the room?* I thought about not getting out of the elevator at all. She was no longer a member, after all, so I could argue that I was no longer her pastor. Besides, I might be the last person on earth she wanted to see.

I walked down the hall, turned the corner, and saw her lying in the bed. Wires and tubes were running in and out of her from machines surrounding her bed, thumping and wheezing their futile soundtrack. She heard my footsteps and raised her head up to see who was standing outside her door. I called her name. She lifted one arm as far as she could, tethered to an IV, and then motioned me to come in. I was still "clenching" at something to say. As it turned out, I never had the chance.

As soon as I reached her bedside, she raised both of her arms off the bed, wires and all, put them around my neck, drew me down to her face, and kissed me on the mouth. "So good to see you," she said. "So glad you came."

For Better or Worse

In our astonishingly superficial culture, we are often very cavalier about things that really matter, while obsessing over things that don't matter at all. Take the vows we say at wedding ceremonies, for example. "For richer or poorer, in sickness and in health, to love and to cherish, until death do us part." In many ways, marriage is countercultural, even un-American. Two people make a public agreement to become *less free.* "From this day forward," they promise *not* to do everything they feel like doing. They pledge, "before God and this company," to be less autonomous individuals, subsumed into a new institution that matters more than either one of them alone—for better or worse. Yet these words have been spoken countless times before family and friends, the "dearly beloveds" gathered to witness what should strike us all as a strange spectacle.

Granted, this is not always what couples *think* they are doing. Sometimes they are obeying what they think their parents want them to do, or society wants them to do, or what seems financially beneficial in a coupled world. After watching couples do this for forty years of ministry, I have a simple rule of thumb. The more elaborate the wedding ceremony, the more expensive, the more obsessed with "perfection," the less chance I give the marriage itself of surviving. There is nothing in a bridal magazine that prepares anyone for real life.

Clergy love to get together and tell wedding stories. There was the time a bridesmaid's hair caught fire (too much hairspray plus too many candles). There was the wedding party that warned me to watch the door for an ex-husband who might show up with a gun. There were family members who instructed me at the rehearsal that an ex-wife must not sit closer than fifty feet from the current wife. I recall thinking to myself, *So what happens if she sits forty-nine feet away? Does she burst into flames?* Or my favorite wedding story of all—the day a wedding photographer punched me in the face just minutes before the ceremony began, as I explained the "house rules." It was a left hook that I never saw coming, and it took me a few moments to regain consciousness. Then I found out that the photographer, who had just been released from a drug treatment facility and was off his meds, had fled the scene and left me to officiate with a fat lip and a bloody nose. I slurred my way through it ("Dearly be-wov-ed") as the mother of the bride wept after calling the police. They don't teach you any of this stuff in seminary.

Despite it all, whether a person believes in marriage or not, weddings are arguably the most obvious example of human beings choosing to surrender the benefits of separation and trade them in for the disappearing act that is covenant. No wonder at bachelor and bachelorette parties, toasts are offered to the bride's, groom's, or partners' "last hours of freedom." It makes marriage sound like a prison sentence, but it's not entirely wrong. It is the prison of self you must escape first. Marriage requires you to consider the consequences of every subsequent action. The days of relative oblivion are gone—more so if children follow—and the field of those whose lives will be changed forever by every move you make expands exponentially. For better or for worse.

I believe this has something to teach us about faith and sin. To live the spiritual life is not to follow orders or to cash in blind obedience for divine favors. Rather, it is to know that no human action is inconsequential. Each and every one vibrates a strand of the Luminous Web and sets in motion changes that we can neither calculate nor predict. If we try to calculate them, especially to our advantage, then we are being selfish. Rather, when we do something good for the sake of goodness itself, trusting in what Dr. King called "the arc of the moral universe," we become co-creators in the redemption of the world. Faith is not about knowing how it all turns out (since certainty requires no faith), but rather about knowing that there are no exemptions from living the entangled life. It's about pushing back against the powerful forces that isolate us from one another; about learning to be honest about our doubts, our joys and sorrows, our fears and feelings.

The poet Wordsworth used to begin his conversations with close friends by asking this question: "What has come clear to you since last we met?" The idea was to dispense with small talk—about the weather, about the news, about the latest gossip. Tell me something that comes from your heart. Not a good or pleasant thing necessarily. It might be the despair you have been feeling because you know that life doesn't get any longer and you haven't been feeling well lately. It might be a discovery about how frequently religion has protected you from the truth, rather than helping you to find and face it. It might be that you are not the person you have pretended to be for your whole lifetime, and now the image you see in the mirror belongs to no one you recognize.

If only we could trust one another to speak this honestly and openly. If only we were not afraid. As it turns out, the devil is not in the details, but in the detachment.

4

Faith as Trust, Not Belief

Truly, we live with mysteries too marvelous
to be understood.

—MARY OLIVER

To be the pastor of the same church for thirty-five years is unheard of these days. Especially if one is a progressive pastor, and the congregation is in Oklahoma City. It makes my colleagues scratch their heads. "Why didn't you move on, Robin?" they ask, with just a hint of incredulous sorrow in their voices.

"Move on to where?" I reply. "To some perfect church without parishioners who drive you crazy? Tell me where that is." In the meantime (the most important time, according to W. H. Auden), what better place to do progressive ministry than Oklahoma? It's exciting. Everyone around here says they love Jesus but would have anyone who looked or acted like Jesus arrested immediately.

What's more, for so many of my parishioners, there is a shared traumatic event that informs our common life. It occurred at 9:02 A.M. on the morning of April 19, 1995, when Timothy McVeigh drove a truck converted into a bomb to the front door of the Alfred P. Murrah Federal Building. He parked, lit the fuse, put in earplugs, got out, and walked away. The blast was so powerful that it knocked McVeigh down two blocks away and killed 168 people, including 19 children. It remains the worst act of domestic terrorism in American history.

All of us who lived through that horrible day became a family forged by grief, which is a much deeper bond than prosperity. Countless clergy, myself included, were given the job of meeting families in a local church to deliver the news that their loved ones were gone and that their bodies might never be found. Then we picked people up off the floor and wondered what kind of world this was. On the other hand, the bombing forged a community determined to recover and to reject hatred in all its guises. It put the resilience of our city on display for the world to see and made this a place that I never wanted to leave.

Recently, I asked my congregation to tell me their God stories. Not surprisingly, one young woman in her early thirties remembered that fateful April morning and wrote about how it changed her views on God forever.

Growing up, my family did not consistently attend church. But in high school, we attended a Southern Baptist church in our town. I found myself saying all of the things that I was supposed to say while not necessarily understanding the theology that I was being taught. I was receiving positive reinforcement, however, and I liked that.

This influence, combined with an offer for a softball scholarship, landed me at Southwest Baptist University my freshman year in college. It was at SBU where I took courses in Old Testament, New Testament, and Spiritual Formation.

SBU is located in southwest Missouri, so as an Okie, I was actually considered a minority. One day, in my Spiritual Formation class we were discussing Timothy McVeigh and his salvation. All my classmates were saying that he was in heaven because he was "saved." I asked about someone born into an indigenous tribe in Africa who never heard of Jesus. That person is in hell, they told me.

I was nine years old when the bomb went off. I knew people who died that day, and to put it mildly I could not imagine Timothy McVeigh in heaven, while all the "unsaved" were sentenced to eternal torment.

Later, my professor assigned me a research project on "another religion." I interviewed my friend who was Mormon. As it turned out, there was little desire to learn about Mormonism. In fact, the real purpose of the assignment was to equip us to convert Mormons and save their souls. I was done with religion.

In 2007, I realized that I was gay, and so of course I became an atheist. In Oklahoma, one is either a Christian or one is a Democrat, but never both at the same time. So I became a Democrat. Everyone was appropriately shocked. I was just angry.

Strangely enough, it was Jesus who brought me around. When I heard sermons about his teachings, about his radical hospitality, about the risks he took for justice and peace,

I found myself changing from an angry atheist to a curious agnostic. Then I attended an LGBT event on a college campus and met a happy young woman with a WWJD bracelet and a subtle Bible verse tattooed on her wrist. I assumed she was straight. I was wrong. But she really, really, really loved Jesus. I had never met anyone like her before.

As our relationship grew, deep theological conversations became the norm. They rarely ended in complete agreement but at some point my thinking about God began to shift. I started using "God" and "the Universe" interchangeably. It helped remove the negative stigma that I had come to associate with God as a partisan Patriarch. Energy, Love, a deep spiritual Mystery—they all seemed more believable to me than orthodox God talk.

I learned in graduate school that prayer improves health, but I believe now that it is more about the act *of prayer than it is about "answers" to prayer. It is about surrendering to limitations, about a desire to connect to something infinite and mysterious that makes spiritual sense to me now.*

As my relationship grew, I decided to propose to my future spouse, now that same-sex marriage was legal in Oklahoma. Because I attend one of the only churches in Oklahoma that will officiate such weddings, I invited everyone from both families to attend, knowing that not everyone agreed with our decision.

To say that it was a glorious evening would be an understatement. The power that is released in the Beloved Community when people from diverse backgrounds are brought together by love is astonishing. Those who attended but did not believe in same-sex marriage were among the most enthusiastic in their support for us. They appeared almost startled by their own response, by how deeply they felt the presence of the spirit. As if the integrity of marriage really is about covenant, not gender. That spirit, present when love is present, and able to warm all hearts, is my best definition of God.

Another important spiritual moment came for me when my grandfather died. It was after a long period of suffering, and finally with hospice care. He waited for the arrival of his son and daughter-in-law from Texas. I saw divine design as the family left the room to share a meal, leaving my wife and me alone with a man I dearly loved.

I had long since stopped believing in heaven and hell, at least not in the traditional sense. I believe that heaven and hell must be conditions on earth. But I do believe in souls and reincarnation. In physiology, the human body takes a glucose molecule and turns it into ATP, which is used as energy and then expired in the form of carbon dioxide. Energy is never created or destroyed, but simply changes forms. I believe this about the human soul. I believe that our souls have all lived before and that each time a piece of our soul comes to this earth, there are certain lessons that we are to learn. I believe that our death comes at a time when our work on this earth is done.

Some of my friends told me that such theology is New Age, and lacks sufficient moral imperative and divine judgment. How will we know who is saved and who is lost? Who is to be punished, and who deserves reward? Who has found favor with God, and who is an infidel?

My answer: we don't know.

"So just to be clear," my friends would say. "Your faith is based on not *knowing?"*

"Exactly," I reply.

"If I was absolutely certain, I would need no faith at all."[1]

Preachers talk about faith as if it's a kind of quantifiable certainty about theological propositions. One exhibits a strong faith by being *certain* about religious doctrines, by not doubting them—or at least by not admitting that one doubts them. Those who lack faith ("Oh ye of little faith") appear to have a deficiency, as if suffering from a kind of spiritual anemia. So when life's tragedies strike, those who lack a certain doctrinal blood count may faint for lack of unquestioned belief. Yet if God is responsible for everything that happens, then God must be the author of every tragic moment as well as every joyful one.

In the ninth chapter of Mark's gospel, there is a story about the healing of a boy who probably had epilepsy. The description is remarkably like a grand mal seizure. "Teacher, I brought you my son; he has a spirit that makes him unable to speak; and whenever it seizes him, it dashes him down; and he foams and grinds his teeth and becomes rigid." Jesus is said to rebuke this "faithless generation" and asks the father of the boy how long this has been happening to him. "From childhood," the father replies, so "have pity on us and help us." When Jesus says, "All things can be done for the one who believes," the father cries out, "I believe; help my unbelief!" (Mark 9:17–24, NRSV).

In that poignant line is captured the long history of human beings who struggle with unearned suffering. Faith, we are told, makes it possible for us to overcome the dread that would otherwise result from believing such events are totally random and without meaning.

Jesus performs an exorcism on the boy, and although the boy appears to be dead, Jesus takes him by the hand and he stands up. The writer of Mark's gospel, the first gospel written, represents Jesus as someone with the power to heal and to bring people back from the dead. Today we know that most people who have epileptic seizures recover naturally after a certain amount of time has passed.

The church has long instructed the "faithful" to believe that "with God all things are possible." But in our world, loved ones murdered while at work in a federal building are not raised from the dead. The demons of addiction often never get exorcised, no matter how ardent the prayers. So what is faith? And why do we continue to scold people who don't seem to have *enough* of it?

Life Is a Trip, Not a Destination

Growing up the son of a preacher, the archetype of faith in my Protestant world was Abraham. Called by God to leave his homeland in search of a place where he has never been, by a route he does not know, he leaves behind everything prosperous and predictable to embark on an uncertain and dangerous journey. One can only imagine the conversation with Sarah (then called Sarai) when her husband Abram announces that it is time to pack up and leave.

"Where are we going?" asks Sarai.

"I don't know," he responds.

"How will you know when you've gotten there?"

"Good question."

"What will we do when we get there?"

"Same things we do here, except it will be different."

"How so?"

"I will become the father of a great nation and have many descendants. So many that we won't be able to count them, as numerous as the grains of sand on the seashore and the stars of the sky."

"Who told you this?"

"God."

"Are you getting a different wife?"

"No, of course not."

"Well, it isn't exactly happening here, so I just wondered. Perhaps we get younger as we journey?"

"That's funny."

"Abram, do you feel all right? You look a little pale, and a bit lost."

"Exactly. Let's go."

How strange, when you consider what the word "faith" now means in most American churches. The father and mother of the three great Abrahamic traditions (Judaism, Christianity, and Islam) based their faith not on a belief system but on a *journey*. Granted, most of us would nod and say, "This is a lovely idea; I enjoy a good journey." But what that really means is that we love to take a trip we have planned, carrying a map (or, now, guided by the surreal patience of Apple's perfect woman, Siri)—with the assurance that when the time comes, we can go back home. It's like camping. As we all know, camping is fun because it is *temporary*. When the tent gets wet and the crackers get soggy, we can pack up, head to the house, and take a nice hot shower.

This is not what Abram and Sarai did. Abram was wealthy and successful and had everything a man could want, except a son. This would be a disappointment today, but in those days it was a crisis of the first magnitude. Children were God's surest sign of favor, not to mention help for parents in old age and a guarantee that the tribe would survive. In a culture that was profoundly patriarchal, sons counted for more than daughters, of course, and being childless was always thought to be the woman's fault. She is barren; let us not worry about whether he is impotent.

So just imagine it. In the shadows of the evening, Sarai would look at the nursery that she had long made ready. There was a tiny crib in the corner of an empty room. Across it stretched one of those mobiles for visual stimulation. It was pink and blue, just to be safe. But across it also stretched cobwebs. When Sarai went to the back door and called out, "Supper's ready, everyone!" only Abram came running.

When I heard this story in Sunday school, I just assumed that they both knew exactly how it was going to turn out. God had spoken clearly and dependably, and in Hebrew no less. What I never considered was the story from Sarai's point of view. She might not have been so fond of wandering as Abram was. She might have thought to herself, *Wouldn't it be nice to get out the good china and build some equity in the house? Now it is Styrofoam cups and paper plates, night after night, not to mention the dust on the floor of the tent.* Dust—life's great guarantee. Like the Okies who lived through the Dust Bowl, you could never get it all out of the house, until it swallowed you up. Then the preacher would sprinkle a handful of it on your grave and say, "Ashes to ashes, dust to dust." This may be the truest thing that any preacher ever says.

It also never occurred to me as a child that faith was anything other than *believing*. We were told to believe in the Bible, believe in Jesus, believe in God, but not once did anyone say, "Trust in the journey." As the world has changed, and many of our beliefs have been called into question, a kind of insidious bargain has been struck in the minds of those who still want to call themselves Christians. They doubt what they are asked to believe but think that faith is what makes it possible for them to suppress those doubts and continue, against the odds, to remain "believers." They hold on to the increasingly implausible claims of the church in exchange for postmortem benefits that may seem equally unlikely. This fragile form of discipleship is really intellectual dishonesty. It is precisely what has permanently propped open the back door of the church.

People often tell me that they wish Christianity were more like Eastern spiritual traditions, which emphasize faith as following a "path" instead of as adherence to doctrines. The irony, of course, is that this is precisely how Christianity started—as a journey, a way of life, not a system of creeds and doctrines demanding intellectual assent to theological propositions. In the beginning, there was no doctrine of Jesus, only the radical *ethic* of Jesus and, after his death, the unforgettable Jesus. Consider this remarkable fact: In the Sermon on the Mount, there is not a single word about what to believe, only words about what to do and how to be. By the time the Nicene Creed is written, only three centuries later, there is not a single word in it about what to do and how to be—*only* words about what to believe.

It often comes as a surprise to people in the church to learn that the first followers of Jesus "survived brutal persecution and flourished for generations—even centuries—*before* Christians formulated what they believed into creeds."[2] Indeed, the evidence is clear that both the appeal and the danger of being what the second-century church father Tertullian called the "peculiar Christian society" was a radical set of behaviors, not a heretical set of teachings. What attracted followers to the Way was the spiritual power of an extended family whose baptism had given them new marching orders. Unlike in Roman and Greek society, the sick were healed at no charge, often just by the laying on of hands. The desperately poor gave up begging, prostitution, and stealing to join a Beloved Community where "sisters" and "brothers" voluntarily contributed money to a common fund to support orphans, prisoners, and those in need.

Early Christians even bought coffins and dug graves to bury criminals whose corpses would otherwise have been dumped outside the walls of the cities. When a plague ravaged the Roman Empire, killing over a third of its population, the only sane response was to flee from those suffering with the disease, all of whom died in agony. But because some early Christians were convinced that God's power was with them, they stayed to care for the sick and dying. A peculiar feature of this "peculiar" group was that they did not seem to fear death.

They believed that God loved the whole of the human race and expected love in return, unlike the gods that surrounded them. "Jupiter and Diana, Isis and Mithras, required their worshipers to offer devotion, pouring out wine, making sacrifices, and contributing money to the priests at their temples. Such gods were understood to act, like human beings, out of self-interest."[3] The early Jesus people were commanded to empty themselves on behalf of others. Although this sounds admirable in theory, in practice it was actually the basis for a radical new social structure.

Rodney Stark suggests that we read the familiar words from Matthew's gospel as if we were hearing them for the first time. They would have shocked the world of Jesus's early followers and their pagan neighbors.[4] They should still shock us today.

> For I was hungry and you gave me food, I was thirsty and you gave me something to drink, I was a stranger and you welcomed me, I was naked and you gave me clothing, I was sick and you took care of me, I was in prison and you visited me. . . . Truly, I tell you, just as you did it to one of the least of these who are members of my family, you did it to me. (Matthew 25:35–49, NRSV)

The gospels talk about God as if the divine were not a distant mystery but an immediate and profoundly subversive reality. "Once Jesus was asked by the Pharisees when the kingdom of God was coming, and he answered, 'The kingdom of God is not coming with things that can be observed; nor will they say, "Look, here it is!" or "There it is!" For, in fact, the kingdom of God is among you'" (Luke 17:20–21, NRSV).

We will never know why Abraham left a settled and successful life behind, except to speculate that perhaps it was no longer satisfying at some deep level. All of us find ourselves wanting to change course, to leave our old lives behind, to strike out on a journey to some new place that promises a new and more authentic way to be in the world. Routine can be both comforting and suffocating. When we leave what is familiar and even lucrative behind in search of what might be more satisfying, this is an act of *trust*.

As Marcus Borg reminds us, the Hebrew word for "faith" in the Old Testament is *emunah*. "[It's] the sound that a baby donkey makes when it is calling for its mother. To appreciate that, you have to say *emunah* so that it sounds like that . . . like a soft braying. . . . There's something kind of wonderful about that . . . an element of confidence that the cry will be heard."[5] In this metaphor, faith is not propositional at all, but speaks to a deep yearning that all of us have to speak and be heard, to call out and receive an answer. Or in this case, for what is vulnerable and lost to be reunited with what means safety and security.

For human beings today the question is not whether this primal need remains but whether the answer comes from a supreme being, or from the people we meet on the journey, or from the deep wisdom of the journey itself. In an inseparable universe, however, it becomes impossible to distinguish one from the other.

Doubt Is Not the Enemy

If one grows up believing the modern distortion that faith is about believing the right things to get the right rewards, doubt will always be cast as the enemy of faith. We talk about people who believe with absolute certainty as "people of strong faith." If they begin to have doubts, we often associate this with temptation, as if the devil has planted doubt in their minds to put them on a slippery slope. "Don't be a doubting Thomas," we hear in sermons after Easter, even though most of us would have to admit that Thomas is one of the most compelling figures in the gospel. Doubt is absolutely necessary in life, even profoundly creative. Because faith is not about believing but about trusting (*fiducia*), the opposite of such trust is not doubt but anxiety. We are anxious in proportion to our lack of trust.

This is not to say that such trust is naïve, or that it protects us from suffering, tragedy, or the certainty of death. Rather, we *lean into life*, sowing the seeds of kindness and compassion and trusting that final outcomes are not ours to arrange but the spirit of God's to complete. This is not a game we are playing, where we act with kindness in order to be rewarded for acts of kindness. That would be a transaction and thus a corrupted form of kindness. If we act kindly in order to receive kindness in return—or even to be thought of as a kind person—then trust becomes a strategy and is therefore not an act of trust at all. What trust requires is not the elimination of doubt but *giving the benefit of the doubt.*

At Mayflower we have an acronym to express this virtue in shorthand. We call it the BOD. "Give the BOD," we often say (the benefit of the doubt), and everyone knows exactly what we are talking about. We are not talking in secret code; we are saying that giving everyone the benefit of the doubt is a cardinal virtue, because it helps us avoid the trap of taking everything personally. I cannot count the number of times I thought someone at church was mad at me, usually because of something they said to me in the line after the service. I went home chewing on it, or letting it chew on me, only to discover that what they'd said had nothing to do with me. Usually it had something to do with what was going on in that person's life, something I knew nothing about.

In the world of church, sometimes the line between the spiritual practice and self-absorption is thin, what Ken Wilber called "the ego in drag."[6] Get over yourself. It reminds me of a favorite aphorism from a good friend. He said, "Before I turned twenty, I didn't care what anybody thought of me. By the time I turned forty, all I cared about was what other people thought of me. Now that I'm sixty, I realize that people haven't been thinking about me at all!"

The simple but powerful idea that faith is not certainty but trust was demonstrated by the woman I would one day marry. When Shawn was a teenager, growing up in a Presbyterian church in Wichita, Kansas, she took a confirmation class and then rebelled. Even at fourteen, Shawn knew she did not believe the creeds that the leaders had them recite. So on Confirmation Sunday, when the entire class was called forward to stand on the chancel and be presented to the congregation as graduates, Shawn remained in her seat and refused to join them.

Needless to say, her parents were embarrassed. When Shawn's mother asked her to explain her "little boycott," this is what she said: "We are going to be asked to recite a creed that I don't believe. If I recite it, then that would make me a liar. You don't want me lying in front of the whole church, do you?"

By some strange twist of fate (or because this is how the Luminous Web works), Shawn would grow up to marry a Congregational UCC minister whose tradition is noncreedal. Thus she would be spared from having to recite a single creed for the rest of her life. Even so, the doubts she had as a child were not a problem to be overcome. They were formative. History is the record of people's well-placed doubts leading to reform. Slavery? I doubt it. The divine right of kings? I doubt it. God as an old man in the sky? I doubt it. If one pretends to believe what one does not believe, then the church becomes an inherently dishonest place. Beliefs may be preserved, as in a museum, but trust is lost. And, as we saw in the previous chapter, when trust is gone, nothing is possible. Ask the countless victims of clergy sexual abuse. Nothing can compare to the shattering of innocence that occurs when someone who represents God says, "Trust me," and then rapes you.

For years, I taught a class at the university called Ethics of Communication. We spent the entire semester studying the rhetoric of deception—in short, *lying*. On the first day, students joked that, unlike in other classes, they already considered themselves experts in this one's subject matter! Over the years, the class grew more relevant, and sometime more painful, as social media grew more pervasive and powerful in their lives. The students recognized that these new freedoms of expression had also created a new kind of chaos. No one needs an editor or a fact-checker to self-publish now. Bullies can work in their pajamas, coming out from under the bridge like trolls to practice the cowardly art of anonymous cruelty. What's more, social media makes it possible for anyone to present an idealized version of himself, airbrushing the ordinary into counterfeit cool. These are not real lives lived by real people. If Søren Kierkegaard were alive today, he would surely call social media the ultimate triumph of illusion.

This insincerity reminds me of the old-fashioned Christmas letter, in which relatives and friends use the birth of Jesus as an excuse to brag about themselves. Once in a sermon I wondered aloud whether an honest Christmas letter was even possible. Not "Suzy has been accepted to Harvard" or "Santa is dropping off the Lexus with a big bow tied on top" or "Johnny was voted most likely to save the world," but instead "Please pray for Uncle Joe, arrested for tax evasion" or "Lisa, who hopes to stay clean after leaving rehab" or "Dominic, who's struggling to save his fifth marriage after being charged with indecent exposure." Signed, "From one dysfunctional family to another, Merry Christmas."

Preachers are always warning us about a world without faith. But what is really terrifying is a world without trust. In that world, we would call everything we disagreed with "fake news." This idea that there is no such thing as truth, only my truth and your falsehood, spells not only the end of democracy and freedom, but also the death of what little credibility remains in the world of organized religion. Countless Christians pretend to be concerned with virtue but then vote as if they are really interested in power. It is a dangerous moment for the human race, because the possibility of civilization itself depends upon a collective commitment to truth and a shared distain for falsehood.

I once heard a story about a snowy night at the turn of the century, when a stranger walked into a church in northern Iwate, Japan. It was Christmas Eve, and he slipped into the back after the service had begun. The pastor noticed that the stranger kept on his hat and cloak throughout the service. After everyone had left, he remained seated, as if waiting for the pastor to come and speak to him. He then removed his hat and cloak, revealing his head, completely shaven and covered with sores. One hand had several fingers missing. The man had leprosy.

"You preached tonight that God is love," he said, looking the pastor straight in the eye. "But tell me honestly: Is God *really* love?"

"Yes, of course," replied the pastor. "I believe it with all my heart."

"Then," said the stranger, "if God is really love, would you be willing to put me up for the night with your family? Please, I have no place to stay."

The pastor was taken aback and begged for time to talk over the matter with his family. "Wait here," he said, and went upstairs to the small apartment above the church where he lived with his wife and two children. There are no guest rooms in a Japanese house, and so an extra mat is laid down for the guest in the same room with the rest of the family. How could he risk the health of his loved ones by inviting in this man? If he himself got leprosy, what would become of his wife and children?

But he wanted to help the man, so for some time he prayed. Then he went downstairs and said, "You can stay here. You can sleep next to me. Bring up your things."

The stranger rose, but instead of going with the pastor, he moved to the door and disappeared into the night. It was reported among the villagers the next day that someone had been causing a disturbance in the streets the night before, shouting, "God is love! God is love!"

Probably some drunk, the people said.

My point is this: Perhaps instead of "believing" in God, our most basic need at this point in history is to experience God. Let the spiritual life consist of those practices that open the door upon new spiritual realities. This does not render God useless. It renders us useful. As strange as it may sound, in an undivided universe, God *is* the field. And stranger still is this idea, namely that *God does not* do *anything, but without God, nothing gets* done.

Born Again to Mysticism

As a child growing up in the Churches of Christ, where musical instruments are prohibited, I seldom heard the word "mysticism," except to warn me about becoming one. Apparently, this was a fate worse than death. Famous mystics were often Catholic, unhinged from orthodoxy, and described with the same vocal inflection that the elders in the church used to describe "hippies." Since I grew up in the sixties and once had long hair, it should not have surprised me when a search committee member in Oklahoma actually put this question to me during my interview for the pulpit: "Are you, or have you ever been, a hippie?"

I stumbled through some kind of answer, but I knew exactly what was bothering those Okies. Like characters in the classic movie *The Graduate* trying so hard to hold their own broken and secretive lives together, what they really wanted to know was whether I might embarrass them someday. Was there a picture of me at Woodstock, for example, or at the 1968 Democratic National Convention in Chicago? Had I smoked marijuana or taken hallucinogenic drugs? Granted, as a straight white male married with two children, I was already at the top of the food chain for clergy employment. But they were worried about surprises. Promise us there will be no surprises.

Looking back, what really surprises me is that nobody asked me a much more important question: "Are you, or have you ever been, a mystic?" You know, one of those strange people with a faraway look in their eye because they have glimpsed the world and everything in it as a sacred unity. What's more, they now understand that unity to *be* God. This sort of trip does not require drugs, but those who take it are often assumed to be confusing enlightenment with altered states of consciousness or mental illness.

Lest we forget, the mental health of Jesus was repeatedly called into question in the gospels, including the infamous passage in Mark 3:21 where his family is said to have gone out to "restrain" him because people were saying that he had lost his mind. The Greek word *existemi*, translated in some versions as "beside himself," actually means "insane" and "witless." The rumors that Jesus was crazy are not just present in the earliest gospel but remain in the last gospel to be included in the Bible. In John, Jesus is described as having a demon (7:20), or as being a Samaritan that has a demon (8:48), which is bad news squared. What I have always wondered is whether this reaction is not identical to those who assume today that all mystics have lost their minds.

Marcus Borg describes two mystical experiences that changed his understanding of God forever. One occurred when he was in his thirties, driving his nine-year-old MG two-seater roadster through a sunlit rural-Minnesota winter landscape. Here is how he describes it:

> *The only sounds were the drone of the car and the wind through the thin canvas top. I had been on the road for about three hours when I entered a series of S-curves. The light suddenly changed. It became yellowy and golden, and it suffused everything I saw: the snow-covered fields to left and right, the trees bordering the field, the yellow and black road signs, the highway itself. Everything glowed. Everything looked wondrous. I was amazed. I had never experienced anything like that before—unless perhaps in very early childhood, and so I no longer remembered it.*[7]

Borg goes on to describe the experience in ways that are consistent with quantum physics and a God who has fallen off the ceiling. "I became aware not just intellectually but experientially of the connectedness of everything," he says.

The second experience occurred two decades later, on a flight from Tel Aviv to New York—in economy class, no less. In the midst of the ordinary routine of yet another long flight, Borg experienced a moment when suddenly everything looked beautiful, including the face of a passenger he described as "perhaps the ugliest person I had ever seen." Even the fabric on the back of the seat in front of him seemed to shimmer. The food tray, the cloud "floor" out the window, stretching to the horizon like an endless cotton prairie, the light that sparkled off an earring worn by a flight attendant. Nothing was too small or too insignificant to remain unilluminated. In a line one might not expect from such a reserved Scandinavian Lutheran, Borg writes: "My face was wet with tears. I was filled with joy. I felt that I could live in that state of consciousness forever and it would never grow old. Everything was glorious, filled with glory."[8]

These are exactly the kinds of experiences that William James described in his classic book *The Varieties of Religious Experience*, published over a century ago. These moments, these mystical experiences, always involve two primary features: *illumination* and *union*. The person perceives some sort of light, radiance, luminosity—or as the prophet Isaiah put it, the understanding that "Holy, holy, holy is the LORD of hosts; / the whole earth is full of his glory" (Isaiah 6:3, NRSV). The second is the feeling we get that we are not separate from this radiance, this luminosity that is God. Such "union" is the true basis of "communion." This is why a closed communion table is such an abomination. Our need for *hierarchy* is the root of our alienation from God. *We take apart what was created inseparable, and the final sin is to separate God from God's own inseparable creation.*

The experience of illumination and union has been described in many ways. Rudolf Otto called this experience of God "the numinous." Abraham Heschel called it "radical amazement." Martin Buber compared "I-Thou" relationships with "I-It" relationships. Abraham Maslow called these moments "peak experiences," while Mircea Eliade called them experiences of the "golden world." Matthew Fox spoke of a cosmic Christ and a cosmic consciousness.

It does not matter what name you choose to call the ultimate reality that is revealed, whether God, Lord, Allah, Brahman, Atman, or countless others. It remains beyond language and impossible to fully express. The common theme, however, is that you experience the mystical when you let the partition between yourself and everything outside yourself fall away. You will feel it when you are not trying to feel it. When you stop walking through your days in search of utilitarian advantages and start seeing the radiance of a world that does not need you. Use the eyes of your heart. When you glimpse this transcendence, even though it is indifferent to you, then you become part of everything that is. Indigenous people have tried to teach us this lesson. When staring into the Grand Canyon, for example, we know the truth. We are saved by the places that ignore us.

Meister Eckhart put it simply: "Theologians may quarrel, but the mystics of the world speak the same language." As

Carl McColman puts it, "Mysticism is, ultimately, simply the art of going to heaven before you die—or perhaps better said, the art of letting heaven emerge within you now."

Leaving the World with Today in My Eyes

Truman Capote once wrote a gorgeous short story called "A Christmas Memory."[9] I share a passage from it at the end of this chapter because it has profound implications for how we think about God, the here and now, and the hereafter.

In it a seven-year-old boy named Buddy has a unique relationship with his eccentric and elderly cousin. She is never named, but she is a devout fundamentalist from rural Alabama, and Capote's description of her is drawn from his own childhood memories. Even though Buddy is very young, and his friend is very old, they have an odd connection—the kind that often grows between innocent souls who love simple things. He loves to visit her, and she loves, among other things, to bake fruitcakes. They have no expectations of each other except to enjoy life. Here is how Capote describes her:

> *A woman with shorn white hair is standing at the kitchen window. . . . She is small and sprightly, like a bantam hen; but, due to a long youthful illness, her shoulders are pitifully hunched. Her face is remarkable—not unlike Lincoln's, craggy like that, and tinted by sun and wind; but it is delicate too, finely boned, and her eyes are sherry-colored and timid. "Oh my," she exclaims, her breath smoking the windowpane, "it's fruitcake weather!"*

She and Buddy gather their own pecans from under a pecan tree, "a heaping buggyload of windfall pecans" that make their backs sore "from gathering them: how hard they were to find," Capote writes, "among the concealing leaves, the frosted, deceiving grass."

He remembers that the old woman has never seen a movie. She would give him a dime on a Saturday sometimes so he could go, but she has never gone herself, and she tells Buddy that she would prefer that he tell her about it. "That way I can imagine it more. Besides, a person my age shouldn't squander their eyes. When the Lord comes, let me see him clear." Later, in the kitchen, they put a little whiskey in the fruitcakes, which is scandalous, of course. Buddy comforts his cousin, telling her she is not old but fun.

For four days they bake fruitcakes, which they send to people they hardly know, including FDR. They drink the remaining whiskey and are severely reprimanded by angry relatives. On Christmas morning, they both rise early to open presents. Everyone is poor, and so Buddy is disappointed to receive the usual collection of hand-me-downs and a subscription to a religious magazine.

What saves this Christmas, and every Christmas, are the kites. Every year Buddy makes one for his friend and she makes one for him—homemade custom kites—because they are both "champion kite-flyers who study the wind like sailors."

That's when they head to the pasture, with the cousin's little dog, Queenie. "Plunging through the healthy waist-high grass, we unreel our kites, feel them twitching at the string like sky fish as they swim into the wind. Satisfied, sun-warmed, we sprawl in the grass and peel Satsumas and watch our kites cavort."

Suddenly, in an epiphany that makes the old woman a mystic, Capote writes about a moment of illumination and union:

"You know what I've always thought?" she asks in a tone of discovery, and not smiling at me but a point beyond. "I've always thought a body would have to be sick and dying before they saw the Lord. And I imagined that when He came it would be like looking at the Baptist window: pretty as colored glass with the sun pouring through, such a shine you don't know it's getting dark. And it's been a comfort: to think of that shine taking away all the spooky feeling. But I'll wager it never happens. I'll wager at the very end a body realizes the Lord has already shown Himself. That things as they are"—her hand circles in a gesture that gathers clouds and kites and grass and Queenie pawing the earth over her bone—"just what they've always seen, was seeing Him. As for me, I could leave the world with today in my eyes."

5

Prayer as Access, Not Petition

JUST ONE GOD

And so many of us.
How can we expect Him
to keep track of which voice
goes with what request.
Words work their way skyward.
Oh Lord, followed by petition—
for a cure, the safe landing.
For what is lost, missing—
a spouse, a job, the final game.
Complaint cloaked as need—
the faster car, porcelain teeth.
That so many entreaties
go unanswered
may say less about our lamentable
inability to be heard
than our inherent flawed condition.

Why else, at birth, the first sound
we make, that full-throttled cry?
Of want, want, want.
Of never enough. Desire
as embedded in us as the ancestral tug

in my unconscienced dog who takes
to the woods, nose to the ground, pulled far
from domesticated hearth, bowl of kibble.
Left behind, I go about my superior business,
my daily ritual I could call prayer.

But look, this morning, in my kitchen,
I'm not asking for more of anything.
My husband slices bread,
hums a tune from our past.
Eggs spatter in a skillet.
Wands of lilac I stuck in a glass
by the open window wobble
in a radiant and—dare I say it?—
merciful light.

—DEBORAH CUMMINS

Pastor Bobby was young and eager and full of intoxicating certainty when it came to what he calls the "power of prayer." He grew up listening to famous evangelists in the Southern Baptist tradition, who taught him by example that prayer should have a certain cadence. The voice should have an endearing, almost adoring breathiness, as if the preacher were astonished to be in the same room with Jesus, but also like the two of them "go way back."

The prayer is often addressed to Jesus, as if Jesus and God were one and the same (a heresy, in fact, says the church, but why quibble?). Most of all, the prayer leaves the impression that you are speaking not to the God of the universe but to an old friend from high school who really knows your wild side but loves you anyway. It is the language of a theological "bromance" mixed with the pseudo-wisdom of "mansplaining," and the congregation overhears this informal chat. Each sentence begins with, "Jesus, we just . . ." But it sounds a lot like "Jesus-Wejus."

Jesus-Wejus want to thank you for being with us this morning, and Jesus-Wejus want to let you know how much we love you, and Jesus-Wejus want to remind you that we know that you know everything—especially that we are all sinners, that we are nothing without you, that we are lost and forsaken without the gift of your redeeming blood! Jesus-Wejus we just want to stop right here, right now, and sign off by telling it like it is. You are Awesome. You are the King! Amen!

This parody often comes up at places where clergy gather, especially among evangelicals who can laugh at themselves. But by no means can progressive Christians be let off the hook. Our approach to prayer has sometimes been called "sneak-a-preach." It goes something like this.

Pastor Jeremiah has just graduated from the Theological Union at Berkeley, and he knows more about what he *doesn't* believe than anyone in the history of the world. He was voted most congenial agnostic by his fellow seminarians. He sports a beard, smokes a pipe, drives a Prius, and tells friends that he is a vegan for Jesus. When he prays, you will need to set aside some time to listen, because he likes the sound of his peace-and-justice voice. His prayers are published with footnotes, but no one would ever describe them as confessional or soulful. Rather, they resemble something closer to a paid political announcement on behalf of the Democratic Party. The politics differ from church to church, of course, but such prayers are often a very long list of "isn't it awful?" grievances. Everyone pulls up a chair, pours one another a big cup of despair, and repeats the great liberal myth: *To have reasoned well is to have acted well.*

Pastor J (as his people call him) must think that God has not received the memo listing each and every resolution that his denomination, the United Church of Christ, passed at its last General Synod. Progressives love to state injustices emphatically, and often self-righteously, as if perhaps prayers are like a white paper read aloud with feeling while people bow their heads. One theologian compared it to sheep getting together to pass resolutions against the wolves. Once the church was revolutionary. Now it is "resolutionary."

In this sneak-a-preach mode of prayer, the minister pretends to be praying but is actually preaching with eyes closed. Here is the sound of Pastor Jeremiah doing a sneak-a-preach prayer:

Let us bow our heads . . . or not.

Unknowable, unnamable, mysterious ground of our being, who may or may not be a meaningful existential reality, we come to you as critical thinkers who believe in evidence-based religion. We suspect that Moses may not have written the Torah, that Jesus did not say most of the things attributed to him in the gospels, and that we would be better off without the book of Revelation. But enough about us.

How long? How long, oh Lord (if we may call you Lord, given its master/servant connotations), will the ignorant and the superstitious prosper in megachurches? How long will intelligent design be taught by the unintelligent? How long before the Supreme Court falls off the right side of the world and robs our grandchildren of their future? How long before Clarence Thomas speaks again? But most of all, pure undefiled mind of the universe, how long—how long, oh Lord—can your servant Ruth Bader Ginsburg last before you call her home? Please, Lord, renew her strength; let RBG mount up with wings as eagles; let her run, and not be weary; let her walk, and not faint! This we ask in case anyone is listening. This we ask even if no one is listening. Amen—or whatever churchy-sounding sign-off you prefer.

Let's Bow Our Heads

My advice to anyone going into parish ministry is to be ready to pray—anywhere, anytime, on any subject. Prayer is such a ubiquitous part of the American landscape that it has become a kind of cultural seasoning, like the black pepper that your server offers to grind over your salad. "Just say amen." In my neck of the woods, almost every important meeting still begins with prayer. Clergy are still asked to offer prayers in the halls of government, even if what happens in the room after the prayer seems profoundly unchristian. Prayer has the unquestioned power to sanctify whatever people are up to, and thus to encourage more of it.

While I was still in seminary, I got called out of class one day to respond to a request from the head of the Chamber of

Commerce in a small Oklahoma town. He said they were looking for someone to pray before the annual rodeo. A rodeo? It sounds easy, but exactly what does one say? Bless the cowboys, that they might be safe? Bless the clowns, that they might protect the cowboys from the bulls? Bless the animals, that they might escape?

Ministers are asked to pray constantly in ways that diminish the whole idea of prayer, especially for or against the weather. "Reverend, please say a prayer that it won't rain on our office picnic," someone asks. But at that very moment, the local farmers are asking their ministers to pray *for* rain, lest they lose the crops that make the picnic possible! "Put in a good word for my aunt Sally as she interviews for a job today," says a friend, even though you don't know Aunt Sally, or whether this job is right for her, or if she is even qualified to do it. "Pray for me to stay on my diet," says a friend at the coffee shop. At the end of the day, the pastor begins to wonder if she is an independent contractor for the gospel, or some kind spiritual bellhop.

There are, of course, those prayers that are requested in moments of real crisis. These are the most difficult and the most important of all. After a parishioner receives word that he is dying of a terminal disease; after a parent loses a child to suicide; after an angry drifter named Timothy McVeigh bombs the Murrah Federal Building in your own city, and nineteen children dropped off at a daycare center that morning are vaporized. Writing a sermon right after the Oklahoma City bombing was a moment I will never forget. I was less than a mile away when the ground shook, and the birds flew away from every tree simultaneously. I thought I had it all under control—that is, right up to the moment when I had to stop, go to the bathroom, and vomit.

Three days after 9/11, many churches put together prayer services and opened their doors for people to stop by and pray. What does one say? Would it be better to say nothing, to just sit in silence and contemplate both the capacity of other human beings to do evil and our capacity to do evil in response? Sometimes it is better to light a candle and give hugs than to fill the air with words that ring hollow, especially when you have just watched human beings dressed for work fall from the sky, including one couple holding hands.

Prayer is often requested at moments when nobody has any idea what to say but it seems that something *needs* to be said. Consider all those movie scenes where people stand beside a freshly dug grave in silence because there is no clergy present. You can't just drop a body into the ground and then start shoveling the dirt back without *saying* something, can you? Usually, after the silence becomes unbearable, someone will say, "Shouldn't somebody *say* something?"

One thing is certain. Ministers will be asked to pray countless prayers over a lifetime, and it may be the most difficult thing they are asked to do. It is not a new dilemma, of course. The apostle Paul said plainly, "We do not know how to pray as we ought" (Romans 8:26, NRSV). The disciples of Jesus said, "Lord teach us to pray, just as John taught his disciples" (Luke 11:1, NIV). They must have watched him from a distance and wondered what he was doing, how he did it, and whether there are certain magic words that must be said. Perhaps John had a more straightforward program of rote prayers with specific instructions, while Jesus seemed to withdraw and pray in solitude. After all, this is the most important thing to remember at a time when prayers are blathered in public and poured over us all like syrup on pancakes: Even though the early church did engage in collective prayer, Jesus counseled us to pray *privately*, in secret, and not to be heard by others (Matthew 6:5–8).

Even if they don't like to admit it, deep down many people have come to doubt the efficacy of prayer. It often feels like little more than a social custom, something to break the awkward silence beside the grave or assuage a little guilt at the Thanksgiving table. Is humanity destined to "outgrow" the habit of praying as more and more people give up the idea that anyone is really out there listening? Perhaps before we can answer such questions, we need to consider what it is we think we are *doing* in the first place when we pray. What, if anything, "happens" to our prayers?

We know that all great religious figures are said to have prayed regularly. Indeed, in the case of Christianity, Jesus is "a praying machine," to quote Mayflower's associate minister. When his disciples go looking for him, they find him all alone and—you guessed it—praying. But we have no record of what he said, or how he said it, other than the Lord's Prayer. Although it appears in several different forms in the gospels, it is the only prayer Jesus ever taught and is universally considered the model for prayer in the church. If that's true, we might need to consider whether we have been doing it all wrong. Consider the words of the renowned historical Jesus scholar John Dominic Crossan:

The Lord's Prayer is Christianity's greatest prayer. It is also Christianity's strangest prayer. It is prayed by all Christians, but it never mentions Christ. It is prayed in all churches, but it never mentions church. It is prayed on all Sundays, but it never mentions Sunday. It is called the "Lord's Prayer," but it never mentions "Lord."

It is prayed by fundamentalist Christians, but it never mentions the inspired inerrancy of the Bible, the virgin birth, the miracles, the atoning death, or bodily resurrection of Christ. It is prayed by evangelical Christians, but it never mentions the evangelium, *or gospel. It is prayed by Pentecostal Christians, but it never mentions ecstasy or the Holy Spirit.*[1]

Crossan goes on to make the case that the Lord's Prayer is a revolutionary manifesto and a hymn of hope. At its core, the prayer calls for *distributive justice* to reign on earth as it does in heaven. What's more, it depicts God as a sort of house-holder who desires that everyone have enough. *Give us this day our daily bread.* You can put an *-ism* label on this if you like: liberalism, socialism, or communism. But Crossan suggests Godism, Householdism, or his favorite, *Enoughism.* The Lord's Prayer is a concise vision of a well-run household, justly administered and shaped by one overarching concern: Do all God's children have enough?

It is common for Americans to fear that we will take from the rich and give to the poor, like Robin Hood, and it will be an affront to those who have worked hard and a crutch to those who would work harder if welfare were not provided to them. This is not an accurate reading of the notion of the householder. As a civilized society, we can't avoid asking the question: What is it that we believe that all human beings should have, without which human flourishing and human dignity are impossible?

This is a political judgment, but don't miss the ethical imperative that it represents. When it is assumed that the marketplace can solve all the problems of life, we also assume that the marketplace works equally well for everyone, and that everyone has an equal chance at success. This is the cruelest myth of all. Distributive justice calls on all of us to make certain that "enough" means that without which we would be embarrassed by our failure to be our brother's (and sister's) keeper.

Our problems with prayer go well beyond understanding the most famous prayers. When people bow their heads in public worship, for example, they often hear one of two kinds of prayers, both of which are found in the Psalms. The first is a prayer of *request*, made either indirectly through lament or directly through petition. The second is a prayer of *gratitude*, which often includes "praise" and "giving thanks." In the American church, I hear far more prayers of request than of gratitude. That is, directly or indirectly, clergy will *ask* God for something, assuming that God has the power to give us what we need but cannot get without God.

These requests are certainly not all selfish, as when Janis Joplin lampooned prayer in her 1970 recording "Mercedes Benz." In that a cappella song, Joplin asked the Lord to prove his love for her by buying her a Mercedes-Benz (her friends all drive Porsches, she must make amends), a color TV ("dialing for dollars is trying to find me"), and a "night on the town."

Sometimes clergy pray for admirable dispositions, like strength, courage, and wisdom to be faithful and obedient Christians. Sometimes the requests are more directly related to what constitutes success in the life of the church or individual members, including prayers that enough money will be raised to meet the budget, or that destructive habits or addictions will be broken by the power of a loving God. Again, the essence of these prayers is that something is *needed*, sometimes something very important, and that God has the power to respond to the request by granting it.

Prayers of gratitude, on the other hand, move away from a transactional model and take the form of thankfulness and praise. If gratitude is indeed the essential religious disposition, these prayers seem less goal oriented and more like a song of astonishment and humility. In a world where people complain all the time, a genuine prayer of gratitude can be a refreshing and moving experience. I once heard someone thank God for the fact that he woke up every morning in a dry house with indoor plumbing. His prayer said nothing about whether he deserved this or, by implication, why others didn't. It said nothing about God's preference for those who enjoy such luxuries or what we should do in response to such good fortune. It just *reminded* me of what we all take for granted.

But if the archetype for prayer in the Hebrew scriptures is Hannah, who "pours out her heart" to God, much of the praying that goes on in churches today is more strategic than soulful. People bow their heads, close their eyes, and then overhear what is more often petitionary than penitential, more familiar than reverential, more contractual than covenantal. Which brings us to the problem that the church now faces. Namely, that an increasing number of people who sit in the pews have largely *given up on prayer*. They comply with the request to bow their heads, but some may not even close their eyes. Some stare straight ahead as if they are registering their own silent protest.

They may be fresh from burying a spouse or a partner, after having prayed for his or her recovery. They may have lost a child, and the world now seems achingly devoid of justice, even of fairness. They may have watched in horror as yet another mass shooting unfolded on the evening news. Then they heard it, ad nauseam, and it rang hollow in their ears: "All we can do is pray." Really? Evil is one thing, but prayer as a way of normalizing evil is quite another.

Where is this God whom the preacher now asks us to approach? Why does my preacher say that with God "all things are possible"? What kind of deity grants the most petty and selfish requests for a parking space or a promotion but turns away when a mother prays for the life of a child in the midst of a famine? Thus sayeth the preacher: "Ask, and it will be given you; search, and you will find; knock, and the door will be opened for you" (Matthew 7:7, NRSV).

Often a well-meaning pastor will say something like this: "When you pray, you must understand that sometimes God's answer is no." Really? That makes sense if the request is to win the lottery, but not if it is to spare a child. If God has the power to answer all prayer but sometimes chooses not to, what does it say about God's priorities? It is hard to imagine a theology more cruel, or an image of God more certain to hasten the death of organized religion.

The desire for a spiritual life is as deep as it has ever been, but our old theological assumptions are failing us. As it turns out, those who struggle with the whole idea of prayer are keeping good company, not the least of which are the Hebrew prophets.

Prayer as an Abomination

Countless sermons have been preached about the power and importance of prayer, but precious few have warned the flock that prayer can become an abomination—even something that God "hates" or "despises," according to the prophet Amos (5:21). Indeed, those we remember for having the clearest vision of God were also the most impatient when it came to prayer. The prophets compared those who speak *to* God with those who speak *for* God. The former often fill the air with pious platitudes or the smoke of burnt offerings, while doing nothing to advance what the latter call the real mission of the faithful, which is to bring God's singular concern for justice and righteousness down to earth. To put it plainly, this situation stinks. Strange as it may sound, Amos, Hosea, Isaiah, Micah, and Jeremiah all make one thing abundantly clear: It is not prayer *and* justice that God demands. Rather, if justice is not being practiced, then God wants *none* of the rest of it: not prayer, not ritual, not liturgy, not sacrifice.

Today the situation is exactly reversed. The preaching, praying, singing, baptizing, etc. is what constitutes "church" in the minds of most people. Justice work is optional, "if you are into that sort of thing." But according to the prophets, justice work is what makes you faithful, and the rest of it is not only optional but, in the absence of justice, offensive! It is no wonder that Jesus, the Jewish prophet, continued to teach compassion over contrition and spent as little time in solemn assemblies as possible. He preached only one indoor sermon that we know of, and it did not end well (Luke 4). After escaping from those who sought to kill him (they loved his diction but hated his dictates), he hit the road and never looked at another order of worship again.

If this sounds like ancient history, it would be good to remember that there are common elements to prophetic anger in every age. When outwardly pious people do nothing to stop an ever-growing gap between rich and poor, as occurred in the long rule of Jeroboam II, prophets like Amos resort to metaphors that are brutal and shocking and, according to John Dominic Crossan, "must have seared at least the ears if not the hearts of his aristocratic hearers."[2]

When we use the word "prophet" to describe someone today, we do so from a safe distance. Prophets really are "visionaries after their time," as William Sloane Coffin, Jr., put it. Had we been their contemporaries, we, too, would have taken offense. In churches that stress positive thinking and worship that is "lovely," consider how popular these words by Amos would be if he spoke them in one of our solemn assemblies:

> I hate, I despise your festivals, and I take no delight in your solemn assemblies. Even though you offer me your burnt offerings and grain offerings, I will not accept them; and the offerings of well-being of your fatted animals I will not look upon. Take away from me

the noise of your songs; I will not listen to the melody of your harps. But let justice roll down like waters, and righteousness like an ever-flowing stream. (Amos 5:21-24, NRSV)

Hosea posts a similar warning when Israel and Syria seek alliances against Assyria's military might: "For I desire steadfast love and not sacrifice, the knowledge of God rather than burnt offerings" (Hosea 6:6, NRSV). Isaiah repeats the theme of justice over empty ritual by demanding that instead of doing burnt offerings: "Wash yourselves; make yourselves clean; remove the evil of your doings from before my eyes; cease to do evil, learn to do good; seek justice, rescue the oppressed, defend the orphan, plead for the widow" (Isaiah 1:16-17, NRSV). Micah presses the same point: "With what shall I come before the Lord, and bow myself before God on high? . . . He has told you, O mortal, what is good; and what does the Lord require of you but to do justice, and to love kindness, and to walk humbly with your God?" (Micah 6:6-8, NRSV).

Because churches today advertise prayer as the answer for everything (pray harder, pray more often, pray "without ceasing"), this is a radical idea. Jeremiah even suggests that if worship is *substituted* for justice, the Temple itself will be destroyed (Jeremiah 7:5-7). Perhaps this is now the fate of the church?

For saying this, Jeremiah was almost killed by his contemporaries, foreshadowing the fate of another Jewish prophet named Jesus. The message is exactly the same: Participation in empty ritual without personal and social transformation is a mockery of prayer. To have expressed a good thought is not the same thing as to have done a good deed—even though we are often seduced into thinking so, said Kierkegaard. To have preached a beautiful three-part sermon series on love is not the same thing as being a loving person, no matter how many people ask for copies of the sermons. To have prayed a beautiful prayer (I have actually heard people applaud following a prayer they liked) is never to be confused with what Rabbi Abraham Joshua Heschel called prayer as mitzvah. This is prayer in the form of a deed. When he returned from the voting rights march led by Martin Luther King, Jr., in Selma, Alabama, in 1965, Heschel said, "I felt my legs were praying."[3]

There are three ways to interpret the prophets' denunciation of empty prayer. The first is to say we should give up prayer altogether and instead work for justice. The second is to say that God wants both prayer and justice. The third is to say that God prefers justice over prayer. Indeed, although "God often speaks of rejecting prayer in the absence of justice, God never speaks of rejecting justice in the absence of prayer."[4] This should give all of us who pray, especially those who pray in public, more than a little pause. It should make us repent.

If it's time to question the idea of God as a partisan monarch living above the clouds, then perhaps such reconsideration of God also requires the reconsideration of prayer. If we are going to ask God for things, they should be things that we need, that everyone needs, and not just things we want. Otherwise we make a mockery of prayer. Better to offer prayers of lament, where we express our sorrow about the world as it is, rather than asking for the world as it should be. A prayer that takes the form of "How long? How long, oh Lord?" after another mass shooting is such an example. Prayers of lament fall on the ear very differently from prayers of petition.

This may be more important now than ever, since we all live in a world of instant and overwhelming communication, much of it flooding our phones and computers with horrific information, not to mention outright lies. To find any peace, to do our work, to be as happy as we can be, we have begun to *accept the unacceptable* as normal and unavoidable. It is both the most understandable and the most dangerous thing happening in our time. Rabbi Heschel said, "Should we not pray for the ability to be shocked at atrocities . . . for the capacity to be dismayed at our inability to be dismayed?"[5] It was this idea that led Heschel to conclude that the primary emotion of the truly religious should be *embarrassment*. To be confronted with the gap not only between rich and poor but between what ought to be and what is.

As dogmatic approaches to religion continue to decline, while the ancient idea of spiritual *practice* grows, what will become of prayer, and what shape will it take regardless of one's particular religious tradition?

One wonders if the purest form of prayer is not absolute *silence*. I once heard Henri Nouwen say at a clergy conference that the spiritual life itself is made possible only when we "hold open empty space." The Benedictine monks, for example, have been teaching laypeople something called "centering prayer." What exactly is this "center" they are in search of? It sounds very much like a God who is grounded in *this* world, revealed in human hearts that show compassion and kindness, a God who is both someplace and everyplace. In the physical world revealed to us by quantum physics, the field is everything, physically and spiritually. You cannot tap the tuning fork of existence anywhere without changing the music of the spheres everywhere. Enlightenment is not knowledge of the correct doctrine but the recognition that just as no physical act occurs in isolation, no moral act is likewise inconsequential. Prayer as a spiritual practice can lift the veil on this reality. As if once you arrive at the "center," you will know you are there, and once you are there, you will not need to ask for anything.

> Prayer should be an act of catharsis, or purgation of emotions, as well as a process of self-clarification, of examining priorities, of elucidating responsibility. Prayer not verified by conduct is an act of desecration and blasphemy. Do not take a word of prayer in vain. Our deeds must not be a refutation of our prayers.[6]

Maturity in prayer, as Crossan put it, is to work *from* prayers of request, *through* prayers of gratitude, and on *to* prayers of empowerment. God is "like the air all around us, everywhere, for everyone, always, and both totally free as well as absolutely necessary."[7] If this is true, then it is the spirit of God *in us* that utters the prayer to begin with; we are not asking for intervention so much as acknowledging that the spirit of God has invited us into collaboration. Prayer moves us across the threshold and into this mystery, which is the beginning of all wisdom and the first step toward the transformation of the world. There is nothing outside us that we need. The depths and the heights are the same. The door through which we pass leads into a room called wonder.

Knocking on Heaven's Door

Let's imagine that you are one of those people who struggle with the whole idea of prayer but also believe that as a spiritual practice it still has power and relevance. Let's imagine that you are hungry for some regular moments of authentic communication, to speak and hear words that are deep, candid, and soulful in a world full of shallow noise and commercial racket. Let's imagine that you might be one of those people who hesitate to bow their heads and close their eyes, who may even cringe at the way prayer has become a form of insider trading. Let's imagine that you are someone who both reads the science section of *The New York Times* and still goes to church, synagogue, or mosque.

Let's imagine further that you know that the three-story cosmology of those who first modeled prayer for us no longer exists, nor does the image of a tribal God make any sense to you. How do you pray? To whom (or to what) are your prayers addressed? And what, if anything, can you expect the "results" of your praying to be?

The answers may lie in the most basic assumptions we have about what prayer is designed to do. The traditional language about prayer, as well as the practice of much public and private prayer, is to *get a message to God*, to make a connection between humans and God, to get a very-long-distance call to "go through," if you will. All the ancient language is about God "hearing" our prayers and about our longing for God to "answer" them. If this does not happen, we are left to deal, as best we can, with "unanswered" prayer.

Unless. Unless there is no "hearing" in the human sense, except by those offering the prayer or listening to it, and no "answer" either. What if prayer is not a transaction to begin with, but rather a profound spiritual practice that changes something about our way of *being* in the world? What if the peculiar *posture* of prayer, the cautious and reverential use of language and the humility that comes from admitting that we will never understand why things happen, conspires to change everything by the simple *act* of praying to begin with? Answers are what humans give. Consequences are what God mysteriously enables. Given the barrage of superficial and deceptive language in our culture, prayer can be one activity that carves out sacred space for authentic and humble communication. In a landscape of lies and hyperbole, a prayer that is honest and "self-emptying" can almost startle us by comparison.

As someone called upon to pray in front of other people, it has always struck me that by addressing words to God, I give people the chance to do one of the most powerful things in human communication. They *overhear*. What is overheard is often not how different we are but what a vast storehouse of common yearnings we share. What is overheard is how much, despite our differences, we all ache for justice, and how universal is our impatience with the way things are compared with the way they ought to be. Hearing ourselves *say* it, or someone we trust say it, is cathartic.

Two central figures in Christendom, Augustine and Kier-

kegaard, both remember seminal moments when they overheard someone else speaking words not addressed to them,
words that changed them profoundly. For Kierkegaard it was
a moment when he was walking through a cemetery late one
afternoon. From beyond a hedge, "he overheard an old man
talking to his grandson beside the fresh grave of one who had
been son to one and father to the other." Neither one knew
that Kierkegaard was on the other side of the hedge listening,
but the Danish philosopher remembers how the "grandfather
spoke tenderly but forcefully of life, death, and life eternal.
The substance of that conversation, not at all addressed to
him, was formative" for Kierkegaard. It persuaded him that
the most powerful form of communication is *indirect* communication.[8] Prayer is the archetype of indirect communication.

For Augustine, it was a moment he remembers in *Confes-
sions*. The bishop of Hippo had been quite the rogue, and into
middle age he was tormented by the tension between the tug
of the flesh and the call of the spirit. He was in Milan, sitting
on a bench under a fig tree, his Bible open but his vision
dimmed by tears. That's when he heard the voice of a boy or
girl calling out from a neighboring house. The young voice
said, "Pick it up, read it; pick it up, read it." The words were
not addressed to Augustine at all. The children were probably
playing a game. But as if indirectly instructed, Augustine
picked up his Bible and began to read: "Let us live honorably
as in the day, not in reveling and drunkenness, not in debauch-
ery and licentiousness, not in quarreling and jealousy. Instead,
put on the Lord Jesus Christ, and make no provisions for the
flesh, to gratify its desires" (Romans 13:13–14, NRSV).

Prayer is a verbalized form of meditation, and the object is not to get an answer but to shift consciousness, to interrupt the mundane, to mitigate selfishness, to admit that we are addicted to illusions of control and infatuated with immortality. This would be prayer as *access,* not petition. Dom Crossan put it well: "Are we praying for God's intervention, or is God praying for our collaboration?"[9]

To return to an earlier metaphor, we need to do less "looking up" and more "looking around." Diana Butler Bass, a scholar of religious studies, reminds us that the simplest things are also forms of prayer. Like walking. Especially walking through your neighborhood. You obviously cannot do that with your eyes closed, but the primal act of walking itself is a form of meditation. "Buddhists have long noted the profound relationship between walking and meditation, emphasizing the harmony that develops between breath, movement, and attentiveness."[10] The beloved Buddhist spiritual teacher Thich Nhat Hanh considered the simple act of walking to be a "wonderful miracle."[11] Is it also a prayer?

I must confess that walking for me is both an act of prayer and the inspiration for prayer. Sunday mornings before dawn is a sacred time. I am usually still tinkering with the sermon, but like clockwork I wake up precisely at 5:00 A.M. Before turning on the computer, I make coffee, dress, and walk through my neighborhood, past the same houses that have surrounded me for over three decades. There is nothing unusual about them. I am a suburban dweller, and they are modest three-bedroom "ranch" houses in the tradition of the American middle class. The larger ones have garages, the smaller ones have carports, and I read bumper stickers on parked cars as I walk by. I am keenly aware of the fear that pervades the age in which I live, and I recognize that there is some risk to being a man walking down the middle of the street in the darkness, even more so if I were black.

Some of the houses have motion-detecting lights that turn on as I walk by. Dogs bark, and the occasional fellow insomniac at work in his garage looks up as I pass by. Our eyes meet and he says hi. I say hi back, but we are complete strangers. In fact, that's what dawns on me before dawn. All these people, living so close, and I will never know them. They are the strangers in the neighborhood, living in houses that I will never enter and living lives I will never know.

Inside those houses where night-lights burn and people sleep are stories as varied and complicated as the Okies who inhabit them. Given the odds, I must be walking past a house where a divorce is under way and where a fight may have just ended in tears. Or a house where a little girl is being abused who is afraid to tell anyone. At one corner, I hear a newborn baby squalling in a back bedroom and I wonder if the mother thinks, as all young mothers do, that she is losing her mind. I imagine dirty dishes in the sink, and utility bills, and piles of unfolded laundry. I see exercise equipment through the window that now serves as a coatrack. I wonder about the hidden things, all the secrets that even spouses keep from each other.

When I return to my study, the smell of coffee has filled the house, the aroma of higher consciousness. Our Labrador retriever, Bond (as in James Bond), follows me down the hall and curls up under my desk with a sonorous moan. I reach down to pet him, and he folds his ear flat and rolls over, legs splayed to invite a belly scratch. The unconditional loyalty of dogs is itself an inspiration (as my wife always reminds me, God is dog spelled backward).

I turn on the computer and think about writing the pastoral prayer. The cursor blinks on the blank page, and I think about all those strangers in strange houses at this strange moment in American history. I also think about God, and what a strange job I have been given: to stand up in front of people and try to tell them the secrets of their own hearts, much less to be honest about my own. With every passing year, as the end of my own life draws nearer, there seems to be an ever-shrinking distance between the utterly mundane and the gloriously transcendent. Even my neighborhood at dawn is a burning bush. So I write a prayer, and I speak it to bowed heads and closed eyes at the beloved community that is Mayflower:

A Prayer for the Forgotten

Holy One, we do not know how to pray as we ought to pray. Sometimes we just list our grievances, but you know them already. Sometimes we ask for favors—to make the budget, to elect the latest savior, to make it rain, to make it stop raining, to win the lottery, to feel superior to those we hate, to advance our portfolio, to add square footage to our house.

But this morning, Lord, let's try something different. This prayer is not a tweet, or a post, or the pronouncement of yet another talking head. This is a prayer for all those people who live in the shadows, who wonder if their lives count for anything. The people whose houses we walk by in the darkness but whose threshold we will never cross, whose faces we will never see, whose joys and sorrows we will never know.

This is a prayer for the forgotten ones, in our neighborhoods, lying abed in hospitals, staring through the bars of a prison cell, sleeping on the cold floor of a refugee camp, digging through a garbage dump for dinner.

This is a prayer of lament for the way the world is set up to care about famous people, powerful people, often cruel and selfish people. Meanwhile the little ones we are commanded to care about are everywhere—hidden and invisible. The teacher who doesn't know if she can afford to keep going, the girl who can't tell anyone about her abuse, the teenager who hears voices in his head and doesn't see the point of living, the spouse who covers once more for her partner's lies.

This prayer is for all the people we don't know, will never know, and will never see on the evening news. Yet the prophets have told us that the forgotten ones are precious, and that either all of us matter or none of us do. Help us, we pray, to turn our gaze away from screens and mirrors and toward the stranger—hold open the door, invite someone new to dinner, speak a word of gratitude—so that the forgotten are not forgotten. After all, they hold the world together, and they are doing the best they can. In the name of Jesus of Nazareth, our teacher and Lord, we pray. Amen.

Normal Day

My youngest son is something of a miracle. My wife, Shawn, and I had decided that raising two children was enough, and we had two, so we discussed more permanent forms of birth control. Being a progressive-minded male, I agreed to have a vasectomy. Twelve years later our son Cass was born. His middle name is Isaac, because, you guessed it, when she told me she might be pregnant, I laughed.

Because his siblings are so much older, Cass is, for all practical purposes, an only child. His brother and sister were gone from the house before he was a teenager, and so they seemed more like his aunt and uncle. For Shawn, this late, impossible child pushed back the empty-nest syndrome considerably. And suffice it to say, Cass seemed to intuit early on that he was something special, and that being "unplanned" is not the same thing as being an "accident."

As older parents, we were also more settled, less frantic, and more comfortable in our skin. Even though we had long known exactly what kids want from their parents—for them to be present without an agenda and to give them more of their time—we started trying to practice what we preached. We took Cass on road trips, on book tours, and on vacations in Colorado where he hiked, and grew strong, and helped me build a deck.

There was one moment with Cass, however, that I will never forget. It was unforgettable because of what he said. It was not what we did, or where we went, or even what happened that night that was unforgettable. It was what he *said*—a single sentence that still vibrates in my soul after all these years. I have never heard anything more innocent, more profound, more poignant, or more beautiful in my life.

Cass was nine—a dark-eyed, dark-haired boy of promise. He was inquisitive, winsome, and given to unchecked outbursts of disarming candor. He loved our Labrador, all things Apple, Star Wars, and just being alive. He was tenderhearted, quick-witted, and, like most children who feel safe and loved, singularly without malice.

His father, on the other hand, was a moving target. I always had another sermon to write, another lecture to prepare, a funeral to organize, a book deadline to meet, tenure to worry about, a student complaint or an angry parishioner to deal with. So I was not always "there," and the kids knew it. At the dinner table, they had a sarcastic way of trying to reel me back in. They would see that faraway look in my eyes and then say, "Earth to Daddy! Earth to Daddy!"

On this particular day, which was just a normal day, I finished teaching and headed home, listening to the radio. The song that came on was, "Cat's in the Cradle," by Harry Chapin—a song that is guaranteed to make all busy fathers feel guilty.

I had heard the lyrics many times, of course, and I knew the thesis: A busy father will miss his son's childhood, and when the son grows up, he will be too busy for his father. As Wordsworth put it, "The child is father of the man."

The only difference was that this time the song got through. Perhaps it was because Cass was the last child and growing up so fast. Or perhaps it was because I knew how busy I was. But on this particular day, this normal day, the song troubled me. "There were planes to catch and bills to pay / He learned to walk while I was away / And he was talkin' 'fore I knew it, and as he grew / He'd say, 'I'm gonna be like you, Dad / You know I'm gonna be like you.'"

At that moment I almost changed the channel, but then, as the father of a nine-year-old, the lyrics got downright personal. "My son turned ten just the other day / He said, 'Thanks for the ball, Dad, come on let's play / Can you teach me to throw.' I said, 'Not today. / I got a lot to do.' He said, 'That's OK' . . . 'When you comin' home, Dad' / 'I don't know when, but we'll get together then / You know we'll have a good time then.'"

I pulled off the road to listen to the rest of the song, even though I knew exactly how it ended. But instead of finding it sappy, I found it true. When I got home, Cass was throwing a tennis ball for the dog and ran to meet me.

"What's up, lad?" I said.

"Just hangin' out, Dad," he said.

"How was school?" I asked.

He shrugged and said, "You know, it was school."

The dog dropped the ball at his feet and looked up expectantly, waiting for another throw—and then another, and another, and another.

Cass smiled and said, "Fetching the ball. It's the meaning of life."

"How many times do you think a retriever will do this?" I asked. "As long as someone keeps throwing it? Until dark? Until he collapses of hunger? Or not until the end of time?"

"The end of time," Cass replied, grinning.

I looked at his face and thought to myself, *This is the most beautiful son.*

"Why don't we eat out tonight?" I said. "What sounds good?"

He looked at me plaintively and replied, "Mom says we're having leftovers. She made that speech again about how leftovers are better than original food. Do you buy that?"

"Not really, but I have another idea. By 'eat out' I mean let's make a fire and roast some hot dogs in the backyard and then finish them off with s'mores."

Cass grinned and said, "Sounds like a plan." Then he got a worried look.

"Aren't fires illegal in the city limits?"

"Only if they're not contained and not used to cook something," I said, trying to sound reassuring, instead of sounding like I was breaking the law.

"I have an idea," I continued. "When it gets dark, we'll build a fire in that old cinder block." I pointed to a spot in the corner of the yard. "That makes it a contained fire, right?"

"Absolutely," Cass replied.

"We'll use coat hangers for roasting sticks, and we'll make sure we have plenty of graham crackers, marshmallows, and chocolate for s'mores. That makes the purpose of our fire cooking something, right?"

"Absolutely," Cass replied.

"Go finish your homework," I said, "and I'll get the fire started."

Wandering around the backyard, I found a handful of twigs and small branches to make a fire. I broke them into small pieces and dropped them into the opening at the top of the cinder block until it looked like a nest with a ragged crown. Cass came out with a handful of hot dogs and all the necessary ingredients for s'mores. He was grinning from ear to ear.

The evening had turned to dusk, and a full moon was rising. We tried to light the twigs, but they kept going out. Finally, with much blowing and the addition of some twisted newspaper scraps, we managed to get a tiny fire going. The conversation turned to the importance of fire, and what might have happened to our ancestors if they couldn't get one started. Cass volunteered to gather a few more twigs.

Then we sat cross-legged on opposite sides of this concrete-block-turned-temporary-fire-pit. Cass rubbed his hands together over it and said, "Nice and hot," his face flickering in the firelight.

"Perfect for cooking a hot dog," I replied.

"Or two," he said, grabbing for the package and retrieving two dogs, slick with juice, to impale on the coat hanger.

I put the open buns facedown on the edge of the block, and it made a perfect toaster. Watching Cass keep his hot dogs at a safe distance from the fire, I said, "Put 'em right in there; put 'em right into the flame. Burn those puppies. Nothing's better than a burnt hot dog from an outdoor fire."

So he did, and they blistered black on both sides and split open, swollen and sizzling. He put both dogs into a single bun and lathered it with mustard and relish. He took a bite, and then he looked around the backyard for a moment as if he were searching for something—as if, even at age nine, he were trying to hold it all. A dollop of mustard was left clinging to his upper lip. I popped the tops off two cold root beers and handed one to Cass. He took a long gulp, and in the quiet of the evening, I could hear it going down his throat. Then he looked up at the full moon.

After a moment of silence, it happened. That's when he said it. That's when he said what I have never forgotten. I can assure you that if he had not said it, I would not be telling you this story after all these years.

"Dad," he said.

"Yes, son?"

"This is the greatest night of my life."

6

Every Move We Make: A Theology of Consequence

Two roads diverged in a yellow wood,
And sorry I could not travel both
And be one traveler, long I stood
And looked down one as far as I could
To where it bent in the undergrowth;

Then took the other, as just as fair,
And having perhaps the better claim,
Because it was grassy and wanted wear;
Though as for that the passing there
Had worn them really about the same,

And both that morning equally lay
In leaves no step had trodden black.
Oh, I kept the first for another day!
Yet knowing how way leads on to way,
I doubted if I should ever come back.

I shall be telling this with a sigh
Somewhere ages and ages hence:
Two roads diverged in a wood, and I—
I took the one less traveled by,
And that has made all the difference.

—ROBERT FROST

If it seems unlikely that quantum physics should have anything to do with theology, consider another well-known scientific theory that crosses over into the world of the spirit. It was made popular by its paradoxical name: *chaos theory*, the idea that there is no such thing as a variable too small to completely change the outcome of complex systems, including human beings—who are very complex systems.

Nearly a half century ago, at the 139th meeting of the American Association for the Advancement of Science, a mild-mannered research meteorologist at MIT named Edward Lorenz stumbled onto a remarkable discovery that he would never describe as profoundly religious. He posed it as a memorable question: "Does the flap of a butterfly's wings in Brazil set off a tornado in Texas?"

Lorenz may never have intended to establish a branch of mathematics known as chaos theory, but his passion for the weather, and his keen power of observation and mindfulness, led him to one of the most intriguing discoveries in all of physics. Although his ideas would be embraced by popular culture, and often misunderstood, not many people thought chaos theory had theological or spiritual repercussions. Most people just remember that a good title is one way to make sure people remember what a scientific paper was about.

What's more, the origins of a scientific theory are often discovered only through unintended consequences. Just as fracking brought the reality of "induced seismic activity" to Oklahoma, Lorenz discovered chaos theory by taking a different kind of shortcut, oblivious to an infinitely entangled ecosystem. He was working on an ancient computer, looking for patterns in the way temperature, barometric pressure, and wind speed, among other variables, could help map weather patterns. All he hoped for was to make weather forecasting easier and more accurate.

He plugged everything into the computer and let it calculate the outcomes. He could see in the graphs how the patterns were affected, but no matter how often he plugged in the same variables, they produced different results and never repeated themselves. The weather did not get any easier to predict; in fact, it seemed impossible to predict, and the more he studied it, the more mysterious it became. Then something amazing happened when he decided to take a minuscule shortcut.

He wanted to look at one part of one sequence in more detail, but he did not want to start the whole run all over again. So he started it in the middle instead, giving the machine its initial conditions by typing the numbers straight from an earlier printout. Then he went down the hall for a cup of coffee. When he came back, Lorenz found a weather pattern so different from the one before that there was no resemblance between the two. He checked his numbers. He checked the vacuum tubes in the computer. Then he realized what had happened.

One of the numbers he was working with was 0.506127. At least that was the number stored in the computer's memory. To save space, the number on the printout was rounded off to 0.506, and that was the number Lorenz had typed in. He had assumed that the difference between the two—

0.000127—was inconsequential, but that was where he was wrong. That tiny number, way down in the millionths—as far as the weather was concerned, a puff of wind no bigger than a baby's sneeze or the beat of a butterfly's wings—that tiny little change at the beginning of a weather system turned out to be the difference between a blue sky and a monsoon.[1]

To this day, the so-called butterfly effect remains a subject of fascination in the public mind, a reminder of the power of unintended consequences. *It is the thesis of this book, however, that such systems also manifest themselves in the world of the spirit.* An act of love as insignificant as the physical effect of a butterfly flapping its wings can end up causing a typhoon of goodness, a tsunami of kindness—or unimaginable cruelty. There is no way to calculate consequences based on how small and insignificant an action is, for good or for ill.

When Rosa Parks refused to give up her seat to a white man on a bus in Montgomery, Alabama, nobody thought that she was launching the civil rights movement. Although she is often portrayed as an innocent instigator, in the wrong place at the right time, new research has revealed her previous interest in civil rights and suggests that she may have been motivated by more than just tired feet. In particular, the news that those who brutally murdered Emmett Till would go free may have put her over the edge when she stepped onto that bus at the end of day.[2]

Even so, she could not have known how it would turn out, and it was a more dangerous move than it was a strategic one. She had no reason to believe that this small act of defiance would be any different from the others, because she had been kicked off this very same bus before. As it turned out, how-

ever, this was the right variable at the right moment. Rosa
Parks sat down, and the whole world stood up. The Montgomery bus boycott was born. Who knows how or why, but
that's where faith comes in. As Barbara Brown Taylor puts it,
"Pick up some stranger's crying baby at exactly the right moment and that baby may turn out to be an artist instead of a
tyrant. Cough at the wrong moment and you may make
someone lose a game of pool on Mars."[3]

This might all seem like a late-night game for science nerds,
but what the world needs now are more theology nerds to
knock on the door and ask to play. When Lorenz helped to
establish chaos theory, the ground had already been shifting
for over a century under the feet of theologians. Darwin's
book *On the Origin of Species* had long ago entered public
consciousness, and religion was still reeling. Scientists were
not only coming up with more and more reasons why things
happen that have nothing to do with God, but also suggesting
that evolution itself is a blind, purposeless process. This idea,
that everything (including human beings) is the result of random variations and mindless chance, is more than just difficult for believers to consider. It is an existential threat. Cornell
biologist William Provine understood this when he said that
the theory of evolution is "the greatest engine of atheism ever
invented."[4]

Perhaps. That is, if one thinks of God as the first and final
cause, a supreme universal agent, first imagining and then *de-
signing* all outcomes in the universe. It is comforting to believe that we exist because God intended that we should
exist. It means we are here in our present form because, as the

poetry of Genesis asserts, humans are the final, consummate project of a creator who had us in mind all along. Chaos theory, on the other hand, suggests that we are a onetime, non-repeatable, fantastic but essentially meaningless occurrence. Go back and introduce even the smallest variable—say, a primate virus at just the right moment in sub-Saharan Africa, or a mosquito bite that brought down a male or female member of the tribe—and your aunt Martha would not exist, nor would you, nor would anyone else you love. A meteor strikes the earth and wipes out all the dinosaurs, or else they might have hung around to snack on humans, and—boom!—there are no dancing feet on Forty-second Street.

Except that this isn't exactly what chaos theory says. It is paradoxically named, because Lorenz believed that results that *appear* chaotic may, in fact, be "ordered" at the outer limits by some mysterious "boundary." You never get the same results twice, but there is also a kind of phenomenological "edge" beyond which those final results never go. Lorenz mapped this boundary and called it a "strange attractor." When he looked at his graphs, he realized that although the weather patterns never repeated themselves, they all traced a pattern that was undeniable, a self-imposed elegance that kept what appeared to be chaotic from flying off the page. Some people have compared this boundary, this strange attractor, to God.

Humans are fascinated by whether there is "order" in the universe, or whether every outcome is completely random. The appearance of randomness, however, may be the result of our limited perspective and the infinite number of variables at work. What appears chaotic, in our lives as well as in the universe, may in the end have an elegant though incomprehensible symmetry.

Chaos theory holds that you can never break a rack of pool balls exactly the same way twice, even if the great pro Willie Mosconi is holding the cue. Why? Because someone in the bar may sneeze at just the right moment and change the barometric pressure in the room. But while it's true that there are an infinite number of possible constellations after a break, you can be reasonably sure that none of the balls will end up hovering weightless above the felt, for example—gravity being a constant variable. What this tells us, as one renowned science writer put it, is that, "no matter how random things may seem, how crazy and out of control, there is a hidden symmetry in them, 'like a face peering from behind the clouds.'"[5]

Every morning my wife and I engage in a simple ritual that seems utterly inconsequential. Shawn eats half a banana and then walks back to my study to give me the other half. She walks up behind me, I turn around, and she hands it to me, the bottom half, hidden beneath the darkened peels that are laid down around it like the petals of a flower. She says, "This is good for you," and I say, "Aha, my half of the banana! There is order in the universe after all." Whatever else may happen that day, this simple act of kindness anchors me. Love, I believe, can act as a strange attractor of sorts, superimposing its own elegant order on what might otherwise seem utterly chaotic and random.

There are other "strange attractors" in our lives—not all of them good. I remember going to see an elderly man in the hospital near the small town of Perry, Oklahoma. I was still in seminary, and he was a member of my student church, but he seldom attended. Now he was dying of cancer. Word had reached me that he wanted "that young minister" to come at once. I knew nothing about pastoral care, but I did know that when a dying person says come, you go.

I stood at his bedside on a warm summer afternoon. We made small talk at first, mostly about the weather and the latest football game. Then he turned to look at me with an intensity I have never forgotten. "Reverend," he said, "I need to tell you something."

"I'm listening," I said.

"I had a housekeeper once. She was Mexican. She was a strong and handsome woman," he said, making the universal sign for a curvaceous woman with his weathered hands. Then his eyes turned back to the window, as if he'd felt a sudden rush of shame. He paused for a moment, and then he said this: "Reverend, I got too close to that woman."

I said nothing and pondered whether this might be the most evasive euphemism I had ever heard. He continued. "Do you know what I mean?"

"Yes, sir," I responded. "I know what you mean."

Driving back home that afternoon, I started thinking about the fundamentals of human existence, the mysterious, outlying "order" of things that do not change from generation to generation—one of which is the need to confess things before you die and ask for forgiveness. I would not have called it a strange attractor in those days. But I would now.

On another visit, this time to a nursing home, I realized that I had the name of the person I was visiting, but not the room number. I did not even know what she looked like. I had forgotten to ask at the front desk, so I found myself wandering down a long hallway, looking into each room as if I would magically know her when I saw her. It felt like watching a slide show of loneliness. Lump after nondescript lump buried under the covers, with no visitors in the room.

Finally, at the end of a long hallway, I looked into a room where a woman was lying in bed with her head back, eyes closed, and mouth open. I just knew this must be the woman I was looking for.

"Are you Betty?" I said, poking my head just inside the door.

She opened her eyes, turned her head toward me, and said, "I am if you want me to be."

We ended up talking for a long time. I never did know what her real name was, unless it was Lonely, a very powerful and strange attractor.

Again, these may seem like random events, but they are stitched together by a common human need. Is there an ache that runs deeper than the feeling of abandonment? Is there a sacrament more profound than human communion? As it turns out, the sacred and the profane meet not in the stained-glass windows that hover over worshippers but in darkened nursing homes where a single word can open the door, pull back the curtains, plump the pillow, and change the face of every nameless person in the world. The word is "Hello."

Science has flattened the cosmos, but *vertical* theology still runs Christendom. Preachers go right on asking God to "come down," to "draw near," instead of telling people that God could not possibly be closer. More of our sermons need to urge that instead of looking to the hills, "whence cometh my help," the flock should try *looking down*, as well as *looking around*. The poet Mary Oliver made a whole life out of such astonished peering. Start with something as "ordinary" as the eye of your dog or cat, and look at it for a long time. Stare at that flecked kaleidoscope that is the iris without blinking, and a portal seems to open onto another universe. The same is true of staring at the center of a flower, the pistil. It seems to disappear like a shutter that is closed over the eternal secret we call fertility.

Don't take my word for it. Darwin was fascinated with eyes (and flowers, too). He said his blood ran cold every time he looked into one. "Trying to imagine how many lucky mutations had to occur in order to come up with one eyeball taxed his faith in his own hypothesis, especially since eyes have apparently developed not once but many times throughout the ages."[6]

Indeed, *consequences themselves* can communicate the deep wisdom of spiritual cause and effect, making angels out of everything that is happening all the time, everywhere—so long as we pay attention. So long as we are mindful.

Once, while riding in the passenger seat with a noted evangelist as he rolled through a car wash, I learned this lesson. A group of young attendants appeared as we emerged from the automated tunnel. They were all teenagers of color, with rags in hand to wipe down his car and keep it from streaking.

"They are like angels," he said as the young men got to work.

"Really," I replied. "Should we tip them?"

"No," he answered. "You don't tip angels. You just let them be a blessing."

I kept my mouth shut, but it made me wonder. Maybe they really are angels, sent to remind us that there is no separation between those of privilege and those who work at the car wash—except for the ways we have chosen to deal with our guilt. He did not even roll down his windows to say thank you or ask for their names. Meanwhile their young brown hands polished the shell around us. We were two old white men in a clean car on a mission to talk about God. But I noticed that my friend never made eye contact with the attendants, nor did he smile, nor did he even attempt a word or two in Spanish.

The moment passed, and those young men slowly disappeared in the side-view mirror as we pulled away. Had we looked at them, had we *really* looked at them, and *seen* them, and *recognized* them—something else would have happened. We would have made human contact across the chasm that separated us by class, race, and language. All the windows would have opened at once, and between us would have passed a tunnel of light. Not the kind that we hear about at the moment of death, but the one that mystics tell us can happen when we are still alive. There are burning bushes everywhere. This is the real miracle. This is the resurrection.

We may not like the idea that we are making or unmaking the world by even the smallest act. But in the world of human chaos, there are just as many opportunities to *reset* any single variable, to change our behavior, even to ask for forgiveness. When we ask people to pay attention to "little things," we are really asking them to pay attention to everything. How small can one change be that saves a marriage, for example, or a friendship, or the planet? Try 0.000127.

There is an old religious word for resetting instead of just rounding off the past. The word is "repent." We think of repentance as the emotional and often guilt-ridden prelude to being born again, but that is because we are immersed in a culture of Christian fundamentalism. The word "repent" has a very simple meaning: to *turn around*. To turn around changes not only the person who turns but also everyone affected by his turning, and everyone affected by everyone who was affected by his turning. This is apparently more than enough to make the eye wall of a hurricane of cruelty break down halfway around the world.

In the language of Frost's poem, consequentiality is captured in the line "Yet knowing how way leads on to way." As one traveler, we may have chosen to marry *some*one, which is exactly the same thing as not marrying *any*one (or *every*one) else. So begins an adventure in which we become, for better or worse, *creators of one another*. We choose a career and begin to think of our identity as being inseparable from what we do for a living (which is why losing a job or retiring can be so difficult). We may have children, planned or unplanned, and thus create not only new human beings who did not ask to be born but immeasurable joy, a lifetime of anxiety, and sometimes unspeakable grief.

To *choose*. This is life's most powerful, most spiritual, most God-like activity. Who among us has not played the game of wondering "What if?" *What if I had not decided to walk into the bar the night I met my wife? What if I had chosen abstinence on the nights when my children were conceived? What if I had fallen asleep at the wheel somewhere on a long drive through West Texas and never lived to write this book?* Benjamin Franklin offered a poetic perspective on a verse that's been around since the thirteenth century:

> *For want of a nail the shoe was lost;*
> *For want of a shoe the horse was lost;*
> *For want of a horse the battle was lost;*
> *For the failure of battle the kingdom was lost—*
> *All for the want of a horse-shoe nail.*[7]

History itself has been constantly reordered by what seem like the most insignificant occurrences. The United States originally planned to drop the atomic bomb on the Japanese city of Kokura, but cloudy conditions made for bad visibility. The bomber passed over Kokura three times before the pilots gave up, and they chose Nagasaki instead. Why? The skies were clear, that's all.

A young Adolf Hitler applied to art school and was rejected, possibly by a Jewish professor. How different would the world be if Hitler had applied himself to watercolor instead of genocide?

When the Cuban missile crisis brought the world to the brink of nuclear war, most people do not know that a Russian navy officer named Vasili Arkhipov may have saved the world. When American aircraft and ships began using depth charges to signal nuclear-armed submarines near Cuba to surface and identify themselves, the sub on which he was riding was so deep that the crew and captain had no idea what the explosions meant, and thought war had broken out. The captain prepared to launch a nuclear torpedo, and everyone agreed with the decision except Arkhipov, who vetoed it. Had the torpedo launched, nuclear clouds would have hit Moscow, London, East Anglia—wiping out half the British population—as well as Moscow and Germany. Even the smallest of decisions add up to enormous consequences, but not because God is punishing or rewarding us. This is the nature of reality. This is the created order. This is what we can depend on, have faith in. We are free to participate, with fear and trembling, in the sublime and terrifying consequences of the Luminous Web, or we can wait to be rescued. When we make what turn out to be good decisions, we can imagine that we deserve our good fortune, or we can turn it loose, grateful for the opportunity to vibrate a single strand of the web for goodness' sake, and then trust, as Dr. King put it, that "the arc of the moral universe is long, but it bends toward justice." Faith is not about believing things to get things. It is about doing what we can, where we are, with what we have.

When bad decisions have consequences, there is always the chance to change course or to ask for forgiveness, both the kind that is offered to us by others and the forgiveness we must sometimes offer ourselves. "Whatever else you have faith in, have faith in this: there is a strange attractor at work in your life that will not let you fly off the page. There is no order without chaos. There is no chaos without order. They give birth to each other, again and again."[8]

Coming Down Off the Mountain

Religion scholar Diana Butler Bass began a discussion of the eternal question "Where is God?" by summarizing how simple and how outdated orthodox theology has become:

> *The church mediated the space between heaven and earth, acting as a kind of holy elevator, wherein God sent down divine directions and, if we obeyed the directives, we would go up—eventually—to live in heaven forever and avoid the terrors below. . . . The Great War caused its philosophical and political foundations to wobble, and the whole thing collapsed after the even greater war, World War II, when the Nazis and the Holocaust and the bomb shattered history.*[9]

In 1916 a young German military chaplain named Paul Tillich found himself in the middle of trench warfare. He confessed to a friend that he spent more time digging graves than he did sharing the sacraments. It was a crisis that caused Tillich to proclaim both his own spiritual death and the death of everything he had once believed about God. What would emerge from that Good Friday experience was the dawn of a radically new way of conceiving of God as the "Ground of all Being." Later Tillich would refine this phrase to "Being Itself." God does not "exist" as other things exist, said Tillich, for all other things that exist were brought into being by something else and will one day not exist. God is not a being with which humans can have a subject-object relationship, even though this is the basis of Western Christianity.

After resisting the Nazis and being the first non-Jewish academic expelled from Germany, Tillich came to America to teach and became a significant public intellectual. He rejected the anthropomorphic "personal God" of popular Christianity but did not deny the reality of God, as did conventional atheists, who often cited Tillich in support of their "God is dead" movement. Like Spinoza, Tillich was a "God intoxicated man" and viewed the disappearance of an inadequate concept of God as the necessary precursor to a grander vision. Tillich's God had fallen off the ceiling.

His public lectures and books reached large audiences, including many people who did not usually show an interest in religious questions. His most widely read books were *The Courage to Be* and *Dynamics of Faith*. In all his work, Tillich argued that the deepest concern of humans drives them into confrontation with a reality that transcends their own finite existence. His discussion of the human situation, and the concept of "ultimate concern," showed a profound grasp of the problems brought to light by modern psychoanalysis and existentialist philosophy.

While much of Tillich's writing is difficult for even scholars to grasp, his effort to define God in nontheistic terms has caused renewed interest in his work today. The shift from God-as-being to God-as-being-itself—present without beginning or end—the eternal residue of the big bang, perhaps, evolving *with* the universe, means that God is not omnipotent in the sense of being coercive. *God cannot force anything to happen, only offer possibilities.*

Without going deeply into this idea, called process theology, it is important to note that this radical theology of consequence was developed as early as the nineteenth century by Alfred North Whitehead and Charles Hartshorne and later was refined by John Cobb and David Griffin.[10] It was a needed corrective to the idea of God as wholly other, restoring the idea of an undivided creation, free will, and the universe as an awe-inspiring and continuous process of self-revelation. Even for those who have never heard of Tillich and will never read a book on process theology, there is an intuitive movement afoot. Millions now believe that God is not "out there" but is, instead, mysteriously "in here"—they say, as they place a hand across their heart and pat some deeper part of themselves. They no longer look up to find God. They look around.

It would be a mistake, however, to regard this as something modern, some enlightened improvement over the mystics who came before us. What is remarkable is how "grounded" our religious traditions were to begin with, and then how hierarchical and stratified they later became. In the Christian tradition, a Jewish teacher of righteousness begins his public ministry by standing in line with other sinners to be baptized, then going into the desert to be tempted and to make a decision—to choose. If we read those temptation narratives as mere theater, in which there was no "real" threat to Jesus (because he is Jesus, after all), we miss the power of everything that came after.

First, if there is no chance that Jesus *yields* to these temptations, then it is a lie to call them temptations to begin with. Second, despite what we argue over today, none of the temptations are doctrinal. They are about *choices*, about priorities for how the kingdom of God is to be made manifest on earth. Third, these decisions are archetypal and formative. They will set the standard for everything that comes after. What should Jesus say yes to? What should he say no to? If our computers operate on a binary language of 0s and 1s, then the spiritual life runs on yeses and nos. This is how you really change the world.

After Jesus fasts and becomes famished, Satan goes right to the most basic need—an empty belly. He says, "If you are the Son of God, command these stones to become loaves of bread." When Jesus answers, "One does not live by bread alone," it would be wise to remember that without bread, one does not live at all. In a land of constant starvation, pierced by the sounds of babies wailing in the night for food, the temptation must have hit a nerve. Why not set up a local rocks-into-bread operation in the desert? Like a first-century version of the food truck, Jesus could run on a platform of food security as an economic messiah.

Next, the tempter takes him to the roof of the Temple and dares him to jump off, to prove that God protects those whom God loves. Jesus refuses to peddle cosmic life insurance and tells his adversary, "Do not put the Lord your God to the test." If this isn't a real temptation, then what is? Just think of the lives that could be saved if only we could depend on faith to grant special favors. People often come to church hoping for protection and shelter from life's chaos, only to find that bad things really do happen to good people.

Finally, in the most American of temptations, the devil takes Jesus to a very high mountain, where he can look out upon all of the nations of the earth and their bounty. Satan says, "All these I will give you, if you will fall down and worship me." That is, I will make you the owner of the whole world, so long as I retain the mineral rights. And Jesus responds with an angry and appropriate denunciation of idolatry, perhaps because even he is tempted by the prospect of such fantastic power. "Away with you, Satan! for it is written, 'Worship the Lord your God, and serve only him' " (Matthew 4:1–10, NRSV).

The closing line in Matthew's account hardly gets any play at all, but if you believe in a theology of consequence, as opposed to a theology of obedience, it is a hidden treasure. "Then the devil left him, and suddenly angels came and waited on him" (Matthew 4:11, NRSV). Really? All it took was a *decision* (or in this case three) to create a moment of bliss? Say no to personal ambition and yes to the kingdom of right relationships? Escape the prison of self by emptying yourself on behalf of others? Make good choices that put justice and mercy ahead of ambition and reputation, and suddenly all the clouds go away and the harp music begins? Actually, yes—it can be this way.

All of us know this feeling, of having confronted our own demons and then chosen to master them. We know the peace of mind that settles into the heart after finally deciding who and what we are and what we will live for. It is a moment too beautiful to describe. Not because all our problems go away. Indeed, some of them will just begin. Rather, it is the liberation that comes from having finally *decided* how we will order our ethical universe. One recalls lyrics from "Teach Your Children" by Crosby, Stills, Nash & Young: "You, who are on the road / Must have a code that you can live by."

Because we have chosen what to *be*, we have also chosen what *not* to be. By choosing what to be, we have chosen *how* to be—which means choosing what to *do*—become a teacher, adopt a child, write poetry, practice patience, keep promises, be present, be kind, be grateful. Those last three (be present, be kind, and be grateful) represent my wife's suggestion for an alternative Trinity. We could do worse.

Not every decision will be right, of course, and every virtue will be tested, but at least some measure of confusion is gone. Joy does not come only in the morning, but also after one has chosen a path and taken the first step down it. What is dangerous in our time is the myth of the "false equivalent." The world is not made up of equally true ideas, and life cannot be lived on the fifty-yard line. Love is better than hate and peace is better than war, because life is better than death. Full stop. Cue the angels.

A Universal Significance

The most important single decision of my life came when I decided that the real question was not *"What* is Christian?" but *"How* is one Christian?" This sounds so simple, even pedestrian, that I am almost embarrassed to talk about it. Of course it matters "how," but let's face it—that word has fallen from grace. Our world values thinkers, not doers, and that means Harvard over the vo-tech. We idealize people who smoke pipes, wear tweed jackets with elbow patches, and sit in conference rooms considering that rarefied thing known as "what." What is the truth? What are the facts? What do we believe?

Witness what happens, however, when someone in the

room dares to ask "how?" As in, *how* do we take *what* we have so studiously discovered and bring it to bear on the world in which we actually live? If some brave colleague dares to ask the "how" question, in a room full of "what" people, you can expect awkward silence, eyes cast down, and the same unspoken question around the table: *How dare you pollute the purity of my what with such a mundane consideration as* how? *We are philosophers and theologians, not mechanics, carpenters, or driver-education instructors. What has skill got to do with the Kingdom of God?*

Such intellectual condescension divides us and can even influence the results of an election. W. Somerset Maugham understood exactly why calling someone a "deplorable" actually makes the world more deplorable.

> *Who has not seen the scholar's thin-lipped smile when he corrects a misquotation and the connoisseur's pained look when someone praises a picture he does not care for? There is no more merit in having read a thousand books than in having ploughed a thousand fields. There is no more merit in being able to attach a correct description to a picture than in being able to find out what is wrong with a stalled motor-car. In each case it is special knowledge. . . . The True, the Good and the Beautiful are not perquisites of those who have been to expensive schools, burrowed in libraries and frequented museums.* [11]

Truth be known, most pastors don't fail in the parish because they do not know *what*. They fail because they do not know *how*. I recall with some panic the first time I was asked to lead a wedding rehearsal and discovered that nothing from my exploration of the Gnostic gospels prepared me to know whether the men stand on the left and the women on the right, or which ring comes first, or how to stop a kiss before it becomes awkwardly long. The same thing happened the first time I baptized a baby. There was nothing in my coursework that had prepared me to know how to hold a baby without dropping it.

Now I believe that everything we do to prepare people to make a difference in the world should be no different from the way we prepare anyone else to negotiate the mysteries of life. We should be teaching them *wisdom*, not doctrine. As for the church, from the cradle to the grave our curriculum should be about *how* one is Christian, rather than about *what* is Christian. Same goes for Judaism and Islam. If we constantly remind ourselves of our differences by retreating behind the walls of dogma, our religious traditions will do us more harm than good.

It has been my experience, however, that the word "wisdom" may conjure up images of know-it-all, self-styled experts telling people (often for a fee) what they ought to do to be successful. But the essence of wisdom, whether it is *sophia* in the Greek and Hellenistic traditions, the Proverbs in Judaism, the *bodhisattva* in Buddhism, or *hikmah* in Islam, has to do with sensing what it is virtuous to *do*, not what it is advantageous to believe.

As a Galilean sage, Jesus belongs in the category of wisdom teacher, not creator and defender of doctrine. Not only did he not announce a new set of rules as a Jewish reformer, but to the contrary, he constantly got into trouble for disobeying established norms, especially prohibitions against blasphemy, working on the Sabbath, and keeping the company of various "impure" human beings—even eating with them.

If you own a red-letter edition of the Bible, try this. With a pen in hand, underline everything printed in red that you think relates to a doctrine (a belief or set of beliefs held and taught by a church, political party, or other group). What you will discover is that Jesus confronts doctrine only to supersede it, especially when it separates human beings from one another. *You have heard it said, but I say* . . . is a radical template for the dismissal of faith as a belief system, now replaced by an ethic, a new way of *being* in the world. So completely has the church replaced the ethics of Jesus with doctrines *about* Jesus that if you ask someone on the street today what it means to be a Christian, she or he will probably begin by listing a set of beliefs. Seldom does anyone begin by saying, "It is a radical and dangerous way of *being* in the world, and a threat to the empire."

This is why a theology of consequence is so radical (in the best sense of the word, to get at the center of things). It does not regard God as a rescuer of last resort, or a religious partisan, or an elector of chosen people, or a real estate broker in the sacred land-grant business. In the church, a theology of consequence chooses the teachings and the example of Jesus and asks for disciples who will imitate those choices in the wisdom of the Way. It does not compel worship through fear or threaten eternal punishment to those who do not believe in the supernatural Christ or man-made doctrines. Incarnation is not a metaphysical reality but a metaphor for what happens when a human being trusts the reality of the Luminous Web so completely that she lives it, loving generously and wastefully without any expectation of reward. When such a God-intoxicated person acts, it almost seems as if God has acted. Yes, exactly.

Not long ago, I received a note from a stranger who works in a large United Methodist Church in Dallas. He said that he was the director of a choir of forty or fifty voices made up entirely of homeless people. They call themselves the Dallas Street Choir, and every singer lives in a shelter, and yet they practice three times a week. They would be in Oklahoma City on a Saturday night, he told me, returning home from a concert in Kansas City. He had heard that Mayflower was a welcoming congregation, and so he asked if we would welcome his choir on the following Sunday morning. I said that of course we would.

There were a few logistical challenges, however. They brought fifty-two singers, and our choir loft holds forty, so we would need to bring in extra chairs. They needed to be on the road home to Dallas by noon, in order to get back into shelters that close at 4:00 P.M., and our second service ends at noon. At first we thought about giving them boxed lunches to eat on the way home, but that didn't sound very hospitable. So we decided to move our worship schedule back an hour so that we would have time for a sit-down meal. Then we realized that if we fed only the choir, the rest of us would be standing around watching them eat. So we decided to do a sit-down meal for the entire congregation and then disperse the choir members throughout the fellowship hall, with church members sitting at their tables for real conversation. Not "Can I get you more iced tea?" but "How did you become homeless? What is it about singing in this choir that is important to you? What do the rest of us still not understand about homelessness?"

Needless to say, it was a morning that none of us will ever forget, not only because their music was incredible (as it turned out, they had performed at Carnegie Hall), but because, to put it in the language of the parable of the Great Dinner, we had every category of those not invited first, "the poor, the crippled, the blind, and the lame," present in our sanctuary (Luke 14:21, NRSV). When the time came to sing a final hymn ("Great Is Thy Faithfulness"), the choir members did not have hymnals. As the hymn started, church members began leaving their pews to come forward and give their hymnals to the choir members. My mostly white, upper-middle-class congregants were creating their own version of the altar call, not to be saved but to share hymnals with a mostly black, homeless choir. It was an unforgettable sight.

The object was true hospitality, and our fear was that the Dallas Street Choir would feel patronized, put on display. So every decision about their visit was shaped by our desire not to "import and display the unfortunate," as our music director put it, and then feel good about ourselves. The text for the morning was Hebrews 13:2: "Do not neglect to show hospitality to strangers, for by doing that some have entertained angels without knowing it" (NRSV). To say that the Holy Spirit was unleashed that morning by a series of *choices* made by the music board is an understatement. They were not earthshaking decisions, but their cumulative effect ultimately shook the earth under our feet. Little things matter. They make big things possible.

As a pastor, I have learned that when people think that the small things they do don't change anything, they stop doing anything at all. I tell them that not every act generates consequences of equal significance but that there is no such thing as an inconsequential act. If organized religion is to survive, and not destroy us, then we will have to recognize that God does not *do* anything. But that without God, who connects all things to all things, *nothing gets done.*

Or consider it this way: *A theology of consequence answers the despair of perceived personal insignificance with faith in a universal significance we cannot see but can depend upon.* When the world seems lost, corrupt, or just bought and paid for, we can give up—or we can remember how unlikely some of the biggest moments in human history have been. The fall of the Berlin Wall comes to mind, predicted by absolutely no one. Someone thought to put wheels on luggage. And the Dallas Street Choir wants to come back to Mayflower because they felt genuine, even radical hospitality.

The truth is that we *can* move mountains. But not if we don't bother to pick up the first stone. It reminds me of a story I heard my mentor and friend Fred Craddock tell once. I was never sure if these things actually happened to Fred, but I knew better than to ask him. He would just smile and say, "Robin, it's not whether or not it really happened, but whether it's true, and is always happening." Not a bad way to read the Bible, come to think of it.

Is That the Same Cat?

Back when families still took Sunday drives, a mother and father and two kids were politely engaged in this American ritual when something remarkable happened. The father was a preacher, and on Sunday afternoons he still had a whiff of that "stained glass voice" when speaking to his children. The kids hated it, because they had heard all his "life lessons" before. Then, suddenly, the daughter started shrieking from the backseat.

"Stop the car! Stop the car! Did you see that kitten?"

"I saw something," the father replied, "but we're not stopping. We're having a nice drive here."

"Stop the car! It's a kitten. I think it's injured."

The big Buick had already rolled well past the kitten, and the father was using one of his favorite tactics—the strategic delay—to avoid a directive. He did this all the time on road trips when the kids were hungry and spotted a restaurant. Driving just past the entrance, he would announce with feigned regret, "Missed that one."

"We're not backing up, kids," he said. "That's dangerous. Besides, that kitten belongs to somebody, and so somebody will come after it."

The brother looked at his sister in horror. They didn't really like cats all that much, but this was a *kitten*. Besides, the mother was looking concerned, so it was three against one. The father's sermon that morning had been about the strange mathematics of compassion, leaving behind the ninety-nine sheep to find the one who was lost. The kids had the old man over a barrel.

"Dad, I think it's dying," the daughter said, shifting into full guilt mode. "Can't we just go back and see if it's OK? What if nobody comes after it? What if it tries to cross the road and gets killed?"

That's when the father hit the brakes.

"Listen, kiddos. We can't adopt any more animals. Do you hear me? There is no room in the inn. Got it? No vacancy. Now, let's have a nice drive, shall we?"

The daughter mumbled from the backseat, "I never thought my dad would just let a kitten die."

This made the father furious. That's when the mother spoke up, and so now everyone knew it was serious.

"You need to go back" she said, "just to see if the kitten is OK. We don't have to take it home, but let's get it out of the road."

The father made a quick U-turn and went roaring back, but he was not happy.

When he got back to where the kitten was, he could see that it was just skin and bones, sore-eyed, and full of fleas—a ragged, mangy little female.

"You kids stay in the car," he said. "I'll take care of this." When he reached down to pick up the kitten by the skin of her neck, she hissed at him and bared her fangs.

Ungrateful little bitch, the father probably thought to himself. *I'm trying to help you here, and you try to bite me?*

He walked back to the car, holding the kitten away from his body as if he were carrying something radioactive. "Don't touch it. Probably has leprosy."

On the ride home, no one said a word. Everyone could hear the kitten whining in the trunk. When they pulled into the driveway, the daughter put on some gloves and retrieved the kitten. She took it into the house, cleaned the pus from its eyes, and gave it a warm bath. Then her brother found a saucer and filled it with warm milk. He set in down in front of this emaciated feline, and she drank it all without stopping to take a breath.

The kids wrapped their now-fragrant little friend in a towel, brought her to the father, and asked if she could stay in the house for just one night.

"Sure," he replied. "Take my bedroom; the whole house is already a zoo!"

They took the kitten to the vet to be examined and get her shots, announcing proudly that they would pay the bill with their allowance. They had no money, of course, but it sounded noble. Then they bought a litter box, an assortment of cat toys, and fixed up a bed out of a cardboard box. The daughter announced that the family could not adopt the kitten without naming her.

"Who said anything about adopting her?" the father snapped back.

"We will call her Aldora. It's Greek for 'winged gift,'" she said.

This was a brilliant approach, given that the father was both a pastor and a professor of English literature. The brother looked at his sister and smiled, as if he had always known the etymology of Aldora. Then he chimed in that she would need a nickname, since Aldora was a bit formal for everyday use. "Let's call her Little A."

Weeks went by, and Little A "grew in wisdom and stature." But no one dared to discuss whether the arrangement would be permanent. The kids put up signs around the neighborhood about a lost cat, but nobody called. They were secretly delighted.

Then one day, they saw it happen. They saw it with their own eyes, even though to this day they have never mentioned it to anyone—especially not on one of their Sunday drives. Their father was sitting in his favorite recliner grading papers and trying to stay awake.

The cat had come in and curled up next to his chair. That mangy little kitten, now a beautiful cat named Aldora, was wearing a rhinestone collar with a name tag. Her eyes were clear and bright, flecked with gold, and her fur was silken.

When he thought no one was looking, he reached down to pet her, but she did not hiss or bear her fangs.

Instead she stood up, arched her back, and rolled her head up to receive his caress. He scratched her between the ears and she purred—a deep, throaty rumble. Then he put down his work, picked her up, and put her in his lap—and the two of them fell asleep.

I am not making this up. The sister and brother saw it with their own eyes. And they both wondered exactly the same thing at exactly the same time.

Is that the same cat?

They looked at each other for a moment but said nothing. There was no need to speak, because it was right in front of their eyes.

That is not the same cat.

No more than any one of us is the same person after someone has found us half dead by the side of the road, picked us up, brought us home, nursed us back to health, and given us a name.[12]

7

The Center of the Universe

Today, from a distance, I saw you
walking away, and without a sound
the glittering face of a glacier
slid into the sea. An ancient oak
fell in the Cumberlands, holding only
a handful of leaves, and an old woman
scattering corn to her chickens looked up
for an instant. At the other side
of the galaxy, a star thirty-five times
the size of our own sun exploded
and vanished, leaving a small green spot
on the astronomer's retina
as he stood on the great open dome
of my heart with no one to tell.

—TED KOOSER

I want to tell you about a place. It is a very important place
to me, even though it will mean very little to most of you.

When I was young, I thought people were important but
places were not. Places seemed incidental, like pins on a map,
or post office boxes, or address numbers stenciled on the curb

in front of your house. Places seemed pedestrian, like squares on the sidewalk that you pass over on your way to somewhere else. I was not "grounded," as they say, and spent all my time looking around things or through things instead of looking at them and really *seeing* them.

Now I know the truth. Whether it's the Promised Land, an apartment in Brooklyn the size of a shoe box, or fifteen acres of prairie grass in the panhandle of Oklahoma with a creek running through it, *place* is what really matters. Remember Abraham? He asked the most poignant and profoundly religious question of all: "Is this the place?" Abraham started out in search of real estate but ended up finding a house whose builder and maker was God.

In my world, one place that matters is a small coffee shop inside an old house in Oklahoma City where for two decades I have gone to wake up, to read, to write, to grade papers, and to talk politics with my friends. At the table where I like to sit and look out the window, there is a small canvas hanging on the wall. It is all black, except for a field of brightly colored stars and a red coffee cup in the middle with a gold band around it, like the rings of Saturn. Not exactly *The Starry Night* by van Gogh, but there is a very interesting caption across the bottom. In simple white letters, it reads, "The Red Cup Coffee House: The Center of the Universe."

A bit over the top, I often thought to myself—until one day, instead of looking up, I looked around. I have always assumed the center of the universe was some*place* else—at some great distance from the earth, of course, and equidistant from everything else around it in all directions like the hub of a wheel.

That is, unless the universe really is infinite, or there are multiple universes, in which case the idea of a center loses all meaning.

Scientists say that the center of our galaxy might be a massive black hole called Sagittarius A*. We can't see it, of course, but it does crazy things to the objects around it, vacuuming up gas giants like dog hairs on a cosmic couch and then making them disappear—or pushing them out the other side into a parallel universe. It is a bottomless gullet of light-devouring gravitational power, a cosmic sinkhole, or a terrifying whirlpool that forms over the drain of the Milky Way, sucking down anything that gets too close. But it's not the center of the universe.

For a human being like me, who cannot be in two places at once (unless there are parallel universes), the real center of the universe is *exactly* where a person finds himself—especially if there is food, conversation, and community. Little did I realize, this funky, eclectic vegetarian café called the Red Cup had been making a spiritually legitimate claim.

Located in the Asian district in Oklahoma City near the university where I teach, the Red Cup is a community masquerading as a business. It is a universe all to itself, a collection of souls who inhabit an old green bungalow where they go to take caffeine, avoid alcohol, and watch the world go by. Over the porch hangs a giant sculpture of a Red Cup, tipped over to spill its sacred java on the heads of all who enter, like the waters of baptism. The Red Cup is a lot like the eighties sitcom bar Cheers, "where everybody knows your name," but with better decor. It was opened and is now run by a recovering alcoholic who is a vegan, a radical environmentalist, and the unofficial pastor of the Church of the Red Cup. Yes, it's also a church. Let me explain.

Human beings need coffee. Human beings need food. Most important of all, human beings need the company of other human beings. We also crave a place in our divided country where "no matter who you are or where you are on life's journey (as my denomination's tagline puts it), *you are welcome here.*" From the moment you walk through the door, no matter how you are dressed, you feel safe and at home. There is art hanging everywhere, and there are books to borrow and read. Look around and you are just as likely to see a prominent lawyer in a silk suit studying a legal brief as you are to see a transgender teenager, or a girl with tattoos from head to toe. You are also likely to see homeless people, both inside and outside. In exchange for working around the café, busing dishes, cleaning up trash, or raking leaves, the owner of the Red Cup will sometimes adopt a homeless person, allowing him or her to pitch a tent on the side porch of the property. The Red Cup even has an urban rooster named Coco. He struts around the parking lot looking to be fed (the owner keeps rooster food on the counter), and he crows all day. If you close your eyes, you would swear you are on the farm, and it is always morning.

When you are there on a cold day, your hands wrapped around a steaming cup o' joe, listening to music ranging from Paul Simon to the latest hip-hop, the words of the Hebrew prophet Jeremiah come to mind: "Am I a God nearby, says the LORD, and not a God far off? Who can hide in secret places so that I cannot see them? says the LORD. Do I not fill heaven and earth? says the LORD" (Jeremiah 23:23–24, NRSV).

So much of our theology in church has been so hopelessly *remote*, along with our concept of God. But humans live in the real world. They walk on streets with real names and love particular people in all their magnificent imperfection. We step on real bugs as they scurry across the floor. We get into real fights and say really terrible things. We worry about real pain that begins in our fingertips and travels ominously up our arm. "What do you think it is, Doc?"

Unlike so much theology, we are not an abstraction. Our lives are not an abstraction. We are not a brick in the wall. In fact, we are not even wired to respond to abstractions. They bore us. What moves us is the power of the concrete and the specific. Angels are not just above us. They are around us and beneath our feet. That's why preachers who peddle harmless abstractions are looking out at empty pews. A minister who talks about the "problem with youth today" probably has no young people in his congregation. When he condemns what is "generally wrong with this world in which we live today, generally speaking" no one is listening, since there is nothing generally wrong with any of us. We don't live our lives in general, love in general, or sin in any general sort of way. We are very *specific* about it. Which may be the last, best hope for Christianity. At its heart, there is nothing general about it, but something very specific, very concrete, and very human. We call it the incarnation.

So where *is* the center of the universe? In a quantum universe, there is no such thing as the center, just points in a field connecting all particular and local webs to the Luminous Web. We are all a system inside a system inside a system, ad infinitum. But if the universe is made up of what quantum theory folks call "nonlocal" stuff, then each of us is both some-place and everyplace at the same time, and we partake in a web of incomprehensible but utterly dependable equilibrium. "What goes around comes around," as they say at the Red Cup.

To claim that a place like the Red Cup is the center of the universe sounds absurd. It is unverifiable and cannot hold up to peer-reviewed skepticism. But once you have been there, you will understand that the claim is not physical but spiritual. This is why I call the Red Cup a church. This little coffee shop is more diverse, more hospitable, and more countercultural than most houses of worship. Sitting at the counter on any given day are evangelicals, atheists, agnostics, and those who are waiting out a hangover. Some are excited just to be alive. Others are thinking about killing themselves. Some are allergic to real church. Others write their sermons at the Red Cup. Some stare at screens, checking to see who "likes" them on Facebook, while others lie in wait to start a conversation that will never end unless you back slowly out the door.

When a member of the Red Cup community dies, there is often a memorial service in the coffee shop. On the counter there is a nameplate next to a stool where a Red Cup regular always sat reading *The New York Times*. He died suddenly and we want to remember him as a patron saint. Often customers will choose not to sit there, preferring the empty stool as a tribute. On Valentine's Day, the Red Cup offers those who are not coupled a chance to celebrate Un-Valentine's Day, because a table for one can be hard. On Super Bowl Sunday, the alternative celebration is called Granola Bowl Sunday, and the Cup feeds the neighborhood without a television in sight. Lest we forget, there are few ways to resist the empire that are more effective than the advice of an old bumper sticker: KILL YOUR TV.

Like a balm in Gilead, there is less talk about sports at the Red Cup than anyplace else in the state of Oklahoma. Otherwise, there are few places where one can escape that constant drivel, the hyperbole, the faux urgency of men who speak of the latest trade, or a bad call, or who is really the greatest, as if they were discussing the destiny of nations. In this way, and in so many others, the Red Cup defies the dominant culture and resists the empire with more than just a hashtag, a "like," a "share," or even a really good sermon.

The Red Cup community does not calculate the odds that it is changing the world, or call a press conference to denounce all manner of evil. It simply acts like a certain way of *being* in the world is how you change the world—but only if you don't spend too much time thinking about it. People will know it when they see it, and then they will pass it along. It gives new meaning to an old line from scripture: "Give, and it will be given to you. A good measure, pressed down, shaken together, running over, will be put into your lap; for the measure you give will be the measure you get back" (Luke 6:38, NRSV).

If you look closely, without blinking and without judgment, there are moments when everyone and everything at the Red Cup seems full of light. "Luminescent," as Annie Dillard puts it, "transfigured" as the Bible puts it. Conversation and laughter around a table create energy that wafts through the room like a breeze. Smiles are contagious, like joy. Sadness is a visitor, too.

What kind of place is this? It is the center of the universe. When you go there, you should take off your shoes, because you are standing on holy ground. Sadly, most churches are not this diverse. The sign out front says ALL ARE WELCOME, but the reality inside is too often a contradiction. Even some communion tables are closed, so seekers go elsewhere—because you cannot manufacture hospitality. You have to practice it.

The center of the universe is that place where the division between the sacred and the profane breaks down. Here is the bread and here is the Red Cup.

There are times when I have sat in this funky café reading the poetry of Mary Oliver and watching the snow fall, and realized that the notion of a God who is someplace else, *any-place* else, seems absurd. If this is not what God intended, then we should live in some other kind of world—a world in which everyone lives abstract lives doing abstract work loving abstract people and worshipping an abstract Deity. Otherwise the long-held distinction between the sacred and the profane is itself profane. The Red Cup is both. It is both local and nonlocal in a quantum kind of way. It really is the center of the universe.

Only the Bound Are Free

To live in America at a time like this, described by some as "late-stage capitalism," is to be reminded that societies can recover from almost anything except too much prosperity for too few people and the death of the common good. So, if a stranger were to approach me on the street and ask, "Reverend, what is the biggest problem facing our society?" I would not hesitate to answer. It is *greed*—the demon stepchild of all the other deadly sins. It is the cancer of never-ending *want* in all its malignant guises, unleashed by the narcissism that is entitlement. This rapacious avarice grows in the space once occupied by empathy. Empathy is a by-product of the moral imagination, which is now on life support. Its opposite, self-lessness or altruism, is the essential virtue of faithfulness. We have made her an orphan in a world where buying and selling is the meaning of existence.

Neoliberal capitalism preaches one message: *I consume; therefore I am*. We are also a celebrity culture that amplifies the voices of people who are well known for being well known, regardless of whether they have anything important, or even coherent, to say. *American Idol* indeed. If Western culture continues its decline, it will be for the myths that destroyed both the common good and our moral obligation to one another—to every single other. These myths abound and go largely unchallenged, especially the myth that the market can solve all the problems in life.

If you dismiss this as a merely political statement, you miss the gravity of it. If you confuse freedom with license to do as you please regardless of the consequences, you insult the sacred meaning of the word. True freedom is about what you *give up* to be in real relationships, not simply what you *get from* those relationships until you are no longer "getting what you need." The most important question was answered long ago. We *are* our sister's and brother's keeper. Although we celebrate the cult of the rugged individual, the self-made man, and the lone ranger in our culture, the truth is that none of us can live or act alone. Existence itself is so fantastically interconnected that when we try to "go it alone," we do damage to ourselves and to everyone around us.

In the 1990s Joan Osborne sang, "What if God was one of us? / Just a slob like one of us / Just a stranger on the bus / Tryin' to make his way home?" The idea was thought to be radical and suggested that we might actually meet God in human form and not know it. Even so, if we did recognize God as a stranger on the bus, this God would then demand that we believe all sorts of things that we might not otherwise believe. A theology of consequence, on the other hand, suggests something much more radical than this. Namely, what if God is *all* of us?

A wise reader might say, "But this is just pantheism, where God is everything and everything is God." I would say yes, but also that God is more than this. The theological term for an omnipresent God is "immanence" (everywhere present), but God is also described as "transcendence" (beyond any single thing). This distinction disappears, however, in a theology of consequence. In a quantum universe, the ideas of local and nonlocal are merged in a field where "here" is "everywhere" and "everywhere" is "here." God is never *someplace else*, even as God is the *totality* of the interface between any one thing and all things. God is immanent and transcendent. God is pure relationship. Perhaps the best word we have for this is "panentheism" (literally "everything is in God," even as God is "more" than everything).[1]

This is what Dr. Martin Luther King, Jr., wrote about from a jail cell when eight white Alabama clergymen criticized him for inciting violence and for being an "outside agitator." Using the margins of the newspaper to write what is now a revered artifact of the civil rights era, King's response to the "concern" of his fellow clergy—now known as his "Letter from Birmingham Jail"—is an eloquent defense of our moral duty to resist unjust laws.

Dr. King explained why time is never on the side of the oppressed, and why as a fellow Christian he was not an "outside agitator" or an "extremist." Unless, like Jesus, he was an "extremist for love."

> *I am cognizant of the interrelatedness of all communities and states. I cannot sit idly by in Atlanta and not be concerned about what happens in Birmingham. Injustice anywhere is a threat to justice everywhere. We are caught in an inescapable network of mutuality, tied in a single garment of destiny. Whatever affects one directly affects all indirectly.*[2]

Dr. King's "single garment of destiny" is another name for the Luminous Web. There are no boundaries except those we create by the illusion of separation. He wrote, "I am in Birmingham because injustice is here." In other words, it doesn't matter where I live or what is happening "there." It matters what is happening "here" and how it changes everything "there" and "everywhere."

As a white pastor in a largely white church, I feel the sting of Dr. King's disappointment with "white moderates." He confessed that the greatest stumbling block to integration was not the KKK but the "white moderate who is more devoted to order than to justice." Nothing much has changed. Today we hear preachers who mouth platitudes about justice but do not follow through by taking any moral action, lest they offend someone in the congregation. They do not organize, they do not protest, they do not create the nonviolent tension that forces a crisis of conscience by shining a light on injustice.

Perhaps what is most insidious, however, is that they make an artificial distinction between partisan politics and the politics of the gospel. This is the illusion of separation again. "Our message is religious, not political," they say. "We save souls, not the world," they remind us. "Dr. King is not from here," said his contemporaries, so when he came to Birmingham without being invited he became an "outsider," an "invader," a "troublemaker." Such walls are a convenient fiction, and all walls ultimately fail. When white clergy said, "Let Birmingham solve Birmingham's problems," what they really meant was "Leave us alone to not fix them if we choose."

I know of no pastor who has not heard this from members of the congregation: "Leave politics out of the pulpit." If this means avoiding partisan politics, as in telling people whom to vote for, or whose candidate has God's endorsement, then this is wise counsel. But if it means acting as if the gospel does not have its own *inherent* politics, its own set of core values, its own demands that one choose love over hate, unity over division, hospitality over exclusion, and equality over hierarchy, then it is an impossible request to grant.

Every political act has consequences, especially when the definition of politics is appropriately broad: *Who has the power, how is it exercised, and to what effect?* In which case every political act creates advantage for some and disadvantage for others. There are no victimless political crimes. Therefore, as long as our laws and our policies *reflect* our values and *affect* the lives of real human beings, no preacher can possibly be politically neutral. Indeed, this may be the most destructive theological myth in the church: that *faith can be personally redemptive without being socially responsible.*

Easter and the Leaven of Nonlocality

Heaven's Imperial rule is like leaven that a woman
took and concealed in three measures of meal
until was all leavened.

(MATTHEW 13:33, SCHOLARS VERSION)

As a preacher's kid who had to go to Sunday school, I remember how harmless this story used to sound. Paired with the parable of the mustard seed, it struck me as the perfect text for a devotional at a meeting of the Ladies' Guild. A woman is baking bread, and she puts a pinch of yeast in the dough to make it rise. Then she takes it to the church potluck, right? What else could the parable mean? Small things can grow into large things—which my Sunday-school teacher told me was just a metaphor for the church. We started out small, like a pinch of leaven or a mustard seed, and look at us now! Any questions?

What I did not realize at the time, however, was that this harmless-sounding parable is as radical and subversive as any in the New Testament. In what may be one of most authentic utterances of the historical Jesus,[3] this one-liner or "similitude" comparing the kingdom of God to a woman baking bread would have been an offense and a scandal to its original audience. It occurs in the gospel of Thomas (which as a kid I had never heard of) and in the Q gospel (which I had also never heard of). But this places it among the earliest Christian documents, whether real (Thomas) or theoretical (Q). More important, "leaven" is not just another name for yeast. It has a powerful history in the Bible.

In the ancient world, the process of "leavening" frequently stood as a metaphor for moral corruption. Why? Because in their defining event, the children of Israel escaped Egypt by taking their dough *before* it was leavened. Moses gave specific instruction that forbade the eating of leavened bread and even demanded that all leavened bread be cleaned out of the house (Exodus 12:15–17). The Jews, after all, do not celebrate the Feast of the Leavened Bread, but the Feast of the *Unleavened* Bread.

Leaven makes bread rise, but it also makes it rot. It both expands bread and reduces its shelf life. In a religious culture concerned with purity and its opposite, impurity through contamination, leaven made bread swell but also deteriorate, like a corpse, due to fermentation. Leaven had such a negative connotation that the New Testament includes numerous references to it as a corrupting force. Jesus warns the disciples concerning "the leaven of the Pharisees and the leaven of Herod" (Mark 8:15, ESV), Matthew uses the phrase "leaven of the Pharisees" to refer to their teaching (Matthew 16:11–12, ESV), while for Luke it is their hypocrisy (Luke 12:1). Paul twice quotes the proverb "A little leaven leavens the whole lump" (1 Corinthians 5:6 and Galatians 5:9, ESV) (not unlike our proverb that one bad apple spoils the whole barrel), and in his first letter to the Corinthians he refers to the "leaven of malice and evil" and contrasts it to the "unleavened bread of sincerity and truth" (1 Corinthians 5:8, ESV).

Simply put, the word "leaven" was what rhetoricians call a "trigger word." When we translate it as "yeast" in a predominately Christian culture, all the offense is lost. Add to this that in the story I read as a child, it is a *woman* who does the "hiding" (*enkrypto* in Matthew, from which we get our English word "encrypt," meaning "to keep secret by means of a code"), and you have an agent who is disadvantaged by gender, hiding something that is a symbol of moral corruption in a very large amount of flour (about fifty pounds). *She acts against the odds and then waits for a chain of events she cannot control.* This is faith as *trust*, first in the mystery by which yeast makes bread rise, and then in the larger mystery of how the reign of God will someday come. How will we recognize it? *There will be enough for everyone.*

A butterfly she is not, but the woman's story is the spiritual equivalent of the butterfly effect. Her small, quiet deed is an equally insignificant commotion. But as "way leads on to way," such an act can make the earth move under Rome's feet. Pilate's wife, already shaken by a dream (Matthew 27:19), will know that the ground is trembling when she sees rings in her coffee cup.

Every act, no matter how small, hidden, or unlikely, spreads out in the Luminous Web like a virus until we are all infected. If that virus is built on fear and hatred, we will die. If it is built on love, mercy, sacrifice, and equality, we will have life and have it abundantly. The future of religion rests not on the triumph of dogma but on the rebirth of wonder and her twin sister, wisdom. And on places like the Red Cup, which serve up both.

There is nothing in the Christian tradition that so powerfully illustrates this shift in thinking like the metaphor of Easter morning. Every pastor knows that this ancient festival of resurrection and the claims that surround it bring out both the largest and the most conflicted crowd of the year. The Easter sermon is the hardest of all sermons to write. What do you say that hasn't already been said? What's more, some feel compelled to attend because it's "the right thing to do." Others come because family members invited them or promised them brunch. But some are also drawn by a deep sense of the mystery of life and death itself, and want to hear someone say that death does not have the last word.

Granted, there are also guardians of orthodoxy present, people who just want to hear it plain and simple, preferably with exclamation points after every other line in the liturgy: He is risen! They are in no mood for nuance. *Don't you dare explain away this miracle upon which everything hangs,* they are thinking to themselves, *even if the last time you saw me was at Christmas.* Others cringe at the prospect of being told that the corpse of Jesus was miraculously resuscitated by God, disassembled and reassembled like a first-century version of "Beam me up, Scotty." They believe, as my uncle put it, that "when you're dead, you're like my dog Rover—dead all over." Others see the empty tomb as a metaphor, and they see Jesus as a martyr and his disciples as mystics who kept his memory alive by reenacting his final meal and toasting to the mystery of his continuing presence. His was a "death that would not die."[4]

What you really have on Easter morning, in addition to extra crying babies and people who feel profoundly uncomfortable on so many levels, is the oldest and most intractable of human divisions—the eternal sibling rivalry of the older and younger brother. Those who love science and reason and want nothing to do with supernatural claims on one hand, and those who define miracles exactly that way and want nothing less on the other. If his body did not rise, claim the latter, then God has not vindicated him and our faith is in vain. If his body did rise, counter others, then why has every other excavated corpse remained rotting in the ground? What's more, if he came into the world without a human father and left in a tunnel of light on the messianic express, then how does a mere mortal like me follow him? I can't walk across my swimming pool.

But there may be another way to look at Easter—one that offends neither the scientists among us nor the mystics who sit in the church balcony. First, it is important to remember that in a quantum world, not even death can finally separate us from the whole. Physicists call it "nonlocality" and Einstein called it "spooky action at a distance," but one thing is certain. We live in a new physical reality, one in which Werner Heisenberg, who gave us the uncertainty principle, discovered that the more precisely the position of a particle is determined, the less precisely its momentum can be known and vice versa. As Heisenberg put it, "the common division of the world into subject and object, inner world and outer world, body and soul is no longer adequate."[5]

You may wonder what this has to do with Easter, but consider how fluid and entangled this makes what was once thought to be fixed and autonomous. Are human beings particles or are we waves—or are we both, depending on who is taking the measurement and how we choose to respond? This matters because of the way we try to solve our problems in a non-Newtonian world. It brings us to the second important consideration for a quantum view of Easter.

Empires are in the body-removal business. When some-*body* becomes a nuisance, a threat to order and loyalty, a disturber of the imperial peace, the goons come down and get rid of the *body*. When the body is gone, they reason, the problem is gone. Crucifixion was the preferred method for certain high-value targets.

It is also important to remember that crucifixion was not unique to Jesus. It was a common method of state-sponsored terrorism. Its effectiveness is entirely dependent upon the idea that there is no body/soul distinction, which is a Jewish idea, not a Greek one. What's more, the corpse, left hanging on the beam along a busy road and picked over by birds and wild dogs, provided a remarkably effective public service announcement. People would look up and be reminded, in the most gruesome way, that insurrection was a death sentence. The message was clear and terrifying: *Whatever this man did, don't do it.*

Rome was solving its problems in the same way it tried to buy peace, the Pax Romana. It was a negative peace that turned out to be nothing more than an interlude between wars. Our own Pentagon once described peace as a "state of permanent pre-hostility."[6] All empires operate this way. Outbreaks of peace are the temporary consequence of outbreaks of war. But this view of the universe fails to account for the true nature of reality. The same violent action that produces an interruption in violence also sows the seeds of future violence. Vengeance has a long memory. But so does love.

So just imagine that the crucifixion of Jesus was, to Rome at least, a merely bureaucratic matter, a strictly *local* problem. Imagine that somewhere on the desk of a Roman state worker responsible for carrying out the murder of dissidents was a file—call it the Jesus file. Word came down that the Jesus file needed to be "closed." The men who did such work were called in, kissed their loved ones goodbye, and headed to Jerusalem to take care of business. They were professionals, and this is how they talked:

"Is he dead?"

"Yes."

"Are you sure he's dead?"

"Yes, he's dead."

"Put a spear in his side just to make sure. Now pull it back out—that's right. Now he's dead, right?"

"Yes, he's dead!"

"Good. I have noted the time of death as three P.M., and I want you to be especially careful with this one."

"Why is that?"

"Because we are dealing with fanatics. And some*body* may want to put this *body* somewhere else. If we allow this, we also lose control of things. If he's taken down and put in a donated tomb, for example, be sure to secure the area. Put a big rock in front of the entrance, and then two of you need to stay up all night. Otherwise this is a standard job. Wash down the blood, disperse the crowd, and don't talk to the locals.

And for God's sake, don't fall asleep, or sure enough, some-*body* will steal the *body*, and we'll have a cult of the risen *body* on our hands. Got it?"

"Yes, sir."

So it is that mere mortals continue to assume that the way to stop some*thing* is to put an end to some*one*, because everything is local. That's why we still talk about Easter as if it were a local claim made about what happened to a local corpse. Nobody had ever heard of "nonlocality." When the Romans took out Jesus, they applied a local solution, execution, to a local problem, insurrection. But when they tried to close the Jesus file, the spear was like leaven hidden in the loaf. It spread like a virus until what was corrupt was itself corrupted. The reign of an unclean God among unclean people had begun, and it could not be stopped. It was the spiritual equivalent of quantum entanglement. If the "twin" is love itself, and death does not have the last word, then so, too, is the orbit of the entangled followers reversed—set spinning in the opposite direction that is eternal life. The apostle Paul tried to express spiritual nonlocality: "So it is with the resurrection of the dead. What is sown is perishable, what is raised is imperishable. . . . It is sown a physical body, it is raised a spiritual body. . . . When this perishable body puts on imperishability, and this mortal body puts on immortality, then the saying that is written will be fulfilled: 'Death has been swallowed up in victory'" (1 Corinthians 15:42–54).

The church has taken too literally the idea of three days, as if this meant seventy-two hours. But more important still, we have all but forgotten that it was *women* who first intuited the resurrection; without them there would be no church. They went to the grave site with food to perform "lamentations" as part of a ritual called the "cult of the dead," which was banned by Rome for victims of execution (lest these foolish mourners mitigate the full effect of Rome's final solution). The women nevertheless kept their graveside vigils and called forth the spirit of Jesus.[7] They brought bread and broke it with tears. When the spirit did show up, the embryo of the Eucharist took shape as well. Take, bless, break, eat, and remember— spooky action at a distance, indeed.

Real, Live Poor People

When I was a boy growing up in Wichita, Kansas, I was a double P-K: son of a professor and son of a preacher. My home church was a stone neo-Gothic edifice called Plymouth Congregational Church. It was an all-white, well-heeled, fiercely independent bastion of thoughtful conservatives, and my father was its preaching minister.

One night in high school, I was sitting in the church balcony on Christmas Eve and felt something tugging at me. I had no idea what it was, or that it would eventually lead me into ministry. At the time, I planned to play second base for the St. Louis Cardinals.

Outside the sanctuary windows that night, giant snow-flakes were falling—straight down in "solemn stillness" like crystal lace handkerchiefs dropping at midnight. The room smelled of candlelight and pine needles. On the chancel was the crèche that some dead person had donated so it could never be thrown away. On this particular night, I could see from the balcony that someone had put a flashlight under the head of the baby Jesus. You've got to do *something*.

My father gave a Christmas Eve meditation on a woman he had read about in the paper who lived on the South Side of Chicago. Her friends called her Hard-Hearted Hannah. She was poor and had no money to buy Christmas presents for her kids. To protect them, she made up a tale of the untimely death of the patron saint of Christmas and explained to the oldest child that for this reason there would be no presents under the tree.

I will never forget a moment in the sermon when my father attempted to speak in the dialect of a black South Side teen, explaining the situation to his siblings. It was a rare departure for this distinguished professor. His manner was always controlled and professional, but he gave it his best shot.

He said, "Ain't gonna be no Santa Claus. Momma say he die."

In that moment, I experienced what theologians call a "thin place." As if the partition between heaven and earth fell away. As it turned out, the story had a happy ending. Neighbors came to Hannah's rescue, and the kids had a Christmas after all. But what I remember most was that my father had tried, albeit in a clumsy and even politically incorrect way, to *speak himself into someone else*. It worked. But it was all still theoretical. That is, until years later I heard yet another story from the finest storyteller of them all. It reminded me of all the ways we try to help one another before first trying to understand one another.

As a kid in the church youth group, I knew how important it was to put "Christ back in Christmas," and let everyone know why "Jesus is the Reason for the Season." So a bunch of us hatched a plan to spread a little Christmas joy. It was the Annual Christmas Project for the "less fortunate," and not for one minute did any of us think we were being condescending about it.

The plan was simple. We made Christmas baskets for the poor, and then we dared to go into what we called "the ghetto" in those days to distribute them. We were very pleased with ourselves. In fact, we were proud as peacocks.

First we collected money. I don't remember exactly how we got it. Probably a car wash, a rummage sale, or we embezzled from our parents—who knows? But we got the money. Then we called the Department of Social Services and asked, matter-of-factly, "Who are the poor in this community?" They gave us a list of "needy families."

We went shopping for fruit and candy and put them in sacks. Then we put each sack in a basket, tied a bow on top, and put in a little card with a Hallmark verse about the true meaning of Christmas. Of course, we were very humble about it. And here's how we "delivered" the true meaning of Christmas: We'd go up on the front porch with the basket and knock on the door, and when we heard the person who lived in that little shack coming, we'd yell, "Merry Christmas!" and then run and jump back in the car and drive on to the next house. We didn't actually want to *talk* to anybody. We were making deliveries. We were not making contact.

By the time it was my turn to make the drop, the neighborhood had come to feel downright depressing. Some of these places didn't look fit for human habitation. *But that's why they could use some Christmas cheer,* I thought to myself. I walked up onto this one porch and knocked on the door. Nothing. No response. *Nobody's home, I guess.*

Just to be sure, I knocked again. Nothing. *Nobody's home,* I thought—almost enjoying the thought. My friends grew impatient and started honking the horn, but I decided to knock once more before leaving, louder this time.

Just as I was about to turn and walk away, his face was at the door, staring at me through the screen. It was a black face, an adult man, and I had not seen it at first, in the shadows of the evening. He said "Hi!" in a big booming voice.

It startled me, but I stammered out, "Oh, hi."

He said, "What can I do for you?" And I thought to myself, *What can* you *do for* me? *Don't you know that I'm here to do something for you? This is not working out like I planned.*

Then another face appeared. It belonged to a woman and she said, "Hi!"

I said, "Hi."

Then she said, "Won't you come in?"

Come in? I thought to myself. *As in go inside?* This was not working out like I planned.

"Come in? Sure, why not?" Then they introduced themselves.

"I'm Benjamin Johnson."

His wife said, "I'm Claire Johnson."

I thought to myself, *How odd; they have names.* My friends were honking the horn, and I must have been staring into space because Mrs. Johnson interrupted the awkward silence by asking, "And what's your name?"

"Who, me? Oh, I'm Robin Meyers, from Plymouth Church, part of the youth group."

"Oh, yes," said Claire, "that's the big church—beautiful church."

I told her that my dad was the minister there, and she said she had heard of him. Then a little boy appeared from another room, and his mother introduced him. "This is our son Timothy."

He looked to be about nine or ten years old, and he smiled and said, "What's in the basket?"

I had forgotten that I was even holding a basket, and I said, "Oh, here. Merry Christmas!" and I handed him the basket. He took it from me and (get this) he started *getting into the basket.* He unwrapped the paper and started opening the gift right there, instead of waiting until I left. My friends kept honking.

Timothy took out an apple as if he intended to eat it, and then he did something really weird. He got out a second apple, and he handed it to me. He gave me back some of my own fruit. I'm thinking to myself, *Stupid kid. Doesn't know how charity works. He's giving me back my own stuff!*

But what was I supposed to do? After all, I was supposed to be humble. So I took the apple, and I sat down and took a bite out of it and thought to myself, *Well, here I am, sitting in the home of real live poor people with real names, eating out of my own sack.*

But I'll never forget what I learned that day. I learned something as powerful as anything I've ever learned in my life. It shapes my theology, my politics, my family life, and my understanding of God. It sounds simple, until you think about it, and then it is an indictment: *All of us, and I do mean all of us, eat out of the same basket.*[8]

Not mine and yours but his and hers, ours and theirs. No more "What do you people want?" but "What do all of us want to become?" Because however we like to hide it behind slogans of the self-made man, manifest destiny, and survival of the fittest, the truth is we all eat out of the same basket. We all eat together.

The world is not our project, where once a year we congratulate ourselves for our generosity to the poor and pretend that this makes up for all the things we do the rest of the year that keep them poor. We're all in this together. *All of us need all of us to make it.*

The real message of the poetry of Genesis isn't that we are infected with original sin. It is a song of gratitude. God made light, a greater to rule the day and a lesser to rule the night, and the stars, and "God saw that the light was good." Then God made the plants and trees and vegetation of every kind, and "God saw that it was good." Then God filled the sea with fish and the sky with birds and even the great sea monsters, and "God saw that it was good." And God said, "Let the earth bring forth living creatures of every kind: cattle and creeping things and wild animals of the earth of every kind," and it was so, and "God saw that it was good" (Genesis 1:3–25, NRSV).

But then God made something else. Slowly out of the primal ooze of nothingness the God of evolution made a creature who could write poetry, paint masterpieces, and raise Lazarus from death—with medicine as well as with faith. When the poet said that God made humankind in God's own image, it is the only time that God says not "This is good" but "This is *very* good." As the Ephesians letter puts it, "We are God's masterpiece" (2:10 NLT).

This was my father's sermon with flesh on. This confirmed for me that being made in the image and likeness of God does not make us "a little lower than the angels" or require that we knock on heaven's door to ask for special favors. But it does mean that sooner or later when we knock, we will all get invited inside. There we will see the work of God's fingers, the moon and the stars, and we may wonder, as did the psalmist, "What are human beings that you are mindful of them, mortals that you care for them?" (Psalms 8:4, NRSV).

But instead of concluding that we are "a little lower than God," we might consider something that is both more frightening and more empowering: that we are the very image of God, and that our treatment of one another *is* our treatment of God. This God is pure relationship, and when we get invited in, we should not be surprised that there is nothing we have to offer that has not already been offered to us.

Epilogue

Above Us Only Sky

You may say I'm a dreamer
But I'm not the only one
—JOHN LENNON AND YOKO ONO, "IMAGINE"

One of the most beloved and controversial songs ever written is John Lennon's "Imagine." It was written at the height of the Vietnam War, when America was almost as divided as it is now. The chords and the lyrics are a dream, but they call for us to imagine a world at peace without religion.

Not surprisingly, critics on the right called Lennon an atheist, and performances of the song have been banned around the world, most recently in Pakistan, where grammar-school students were forbidden to sing it. "The song questions our belief in God and encourages an atheist mindset," said a prominent columnist. "The school is run by an Englishman and that is where the problem lies."[1]

Whatever one thinks of Lennon, or of schools run by the British, the impact of this song has been enormous. Paul David Hewson, also known as Bono, said that "Imagine" was the reason for his career. After the horrific terrorist attack in

Paris in 2015, pianist Davide Martello drove four hundred miles from Germany so he could play "Imagine" outside the Bataclan theater. Former president Jimmy Carter said that as he traveled around the world, he heard the song "Imagine" used almost equally with national anthems. Strange when you consider that it asks us to imagine a world without countries or war.

As for imagining no possessions, critics pointed out that Lennon drove a custom-painted Rolls-Royce, and so he altered the lyrics to ask that we imagine no possessions, "I wonder if *we* can." He also sang about the "brotherhood/*sisterhood* of man" in later renditions as a recovering chauvinist, admitting that Yoko Ono should have been given equal billing for the song, since it was inspired by her book *Grapefruit*. Nevertheless, the real controversy was his assertions that above us there is *only* sky and that the world would be better off with "no religion."

In the early seventies, Lennon was approached by the World Church and asked to change "no religion" to "one religion," but he refused. Obviously the stakes are high. "Imagine" calls for us to *start over*, not just to "make over" the orthodoxies of our time. The song suggests that we imagine ridding ourselves of those things that are most important to us and deeply at the root of violence and war: nation-states, religion, and possessions—a toxic trifecta that deals unending misery and death.

Of course, one can say that "Imagine" is just another naïve utopian exercise in hopeless hyperbole, birthed in a haze of drugs, free love, and "sticking it to the man." But the same could be said of the words of Jesus in the Sermon on the

Mount. Does he not ask us to stop worrying about food, clothing, or possessions? Was this also just a naïve utopian exercise in hopeless hyperbole, birthed in a haze of baffling parables, free healing, and sticking it to the emperor? The call of Jesus to "consider the lilies" (Matthew 6:28 and Luke 12:27, NRSV) is a call not to look up but to look around. There is nothing that we need "above us"; we should be mindful of the feast "before us." Abundance is the true nature of creation. Scarcity is the empire's propaganda.

What's more, "Imagine" is not a manifesto. It is a call to consider what we often think we are not allowed to consider. When asked whether he was an atheist, Lennon responded that he was not anti-Christ or anti-religion. Indeed, he said that he believed in God, "but not as one thing, not as an old man in the sky."[2] He pointed out that he never said, "Imagine there's no God." So when he called for us to imagine no religion, he meant religion as a system of creeds and doctrines with a long, blood-soaked history of oppression and holy wars.

Even so, the song was meant to be iconoclastic, if not blasphemous—just like his song "Instant Karma," in which "your brother is everyone you meet." Or in the case of this book, where God is all of us. To be clear, this does not amend the God of orthodoxy. It *replaces* it with a God that is more expansive, mysterious, immediate, and mystical. A God who does not hand out favors, or grant land, or punish evildoers, or take sides in war. The loss of such a deity poses an existential threat to the religious franchise. Yet our survival now depends upon the death of Michelangelo's God. He cannot be put back together again, much less reattached to the ceiling of a world that no longer exists. Besides, if this reimagining of God seems blasphemous, then what would you call turning the other cheek or praying for our enemies?

On the thirtieth anniversary of John Lennon's death, an article in *The American Conservative* called for people to "Stop Imagining." What could be worse, its author opined, than a dream of no countries, no possessions, and no religion?[3] Perhaps the answer to that question is exactly the world we find ourselves in now: rising nationalism, rising inequality, and rising sectarian violence.

Conventional religious belief and practice is a powerful habit, so powerful that we cannot "imagine" giving it up. We cannot imagine life without a heavenly monarch. Western civilization, founded on original sin and exclusive salvation, is such a powerful major premise, such a long-running and successful play, that we cannot imagine that the show will ever end—that the curtain will come down. But it is coming down, and besides, the audience is full of empty seats. This is not Chicken Little syndrome. The sky God really is falling.

So where do we go from here? *Is there religion after God has fallen off the ceiling?*

The answer for me is a resounding yes. What's more, the systematic implications of a theology of consequence could make the church not only relevant again, but a powerful source of wisdom and transformation. Once we admit that God has mostly been made in the image of humans, we will know exactly what the novelist Gertrude Stein meant when she wrote about Oakland, California, that "there is no there there."

Though this is often misunderstood as an insult, Stein was referring to what had changed about the town she lived in as a child. She had moved away as a teenager and did not return for almost forty-five years. When she did return, it was a city ten times larger than the community she remembered. She went looking for her childhood home and it was no longer "there." Her comment was not a commentary about Oakland, per se, but about lost innocence and the pain that comes from knowing that, as Thomas Wolfe put it, "you can't go home again."

The time has come to admit the same for organized religion. You can't go home again, and there is no "God there." We live in the age of science; instead of fearing this explosion of knowledge, why not consider it a blessing? Who is to say, as Pierre Teilhard de Chardin put it, that research is not also a form of adoration? While pre-scientific humans located God in what they believed to be the dome of heaven, science has revealed a universe where all the rooms are expanding and where all things are part of One Thing.

If this is true, then the whole theological enterprise must be reconsidered. We are not lost and needing to be found; rather we are deluded and need to be enlightened. We are isolated and need to be reunited. We are not helpless, hopeless, undeserving creatures in search of divine rescue. We are remarkable, hopeful, deserving creatures in search of our true identity. Singer/songwriter Joni Mitchell had it exactly right: "We are stardust / we are golden / And we've got to get ourselves / Back to the garden."[4]

When we pray, we should pray for *access* to this mystery,

not lobby it for favors. The object of life is to become fully *alive*, to wake up, to recover the mystical, to disburden ourselves of the illusion that God will do for us what we refuse to do for ourselves. Richard Rohr, who calls Christ "Another Name for Every Thing," put it this way: "Once we know that the entire physical world around us, all of creation, is both the hiding place and the revelation place for God, this world becomes home, safe, enchanted, offering grace to any who look deeply."[5]

Either the church can consider itself a fossil, and its cathedrals, museums, or it can reconstitute itself with new language and new practice. If *God doesn't do anything, but without God nothing gets done*, the spiritual life will not just be altered; it will be transformed.

Once, when Holocaust survivor Elie Wiesel invited a few hundred ministers to study the book of Job in a Jewish temple in Birmingham, Michigan, I was lucky enough to be in the audience. I will never forget Wiesel's opening line. He turned to the first chapter of this beautiful and enigmatic book and said, "First of all, Job was a Gentile. Any Jew would have gotten a second opinion." After the laughter died away, he said something I have never forgotten. He said, "I will not try to convert you to Judaism today, and I would appreciate it very much if you will not try to convert me to Christianity. What I am doing here is trying to be the best Jew I can be, so that you will be the best Christian you can be. Let's study together."

Deep Water

To close, let me tell you something that is true, and yet so remarkable, so "miraculous," that no exaggeration is necessary. Over two decades ago I preached a sermon at Mayflower called "Deep Water." It was based on Luke's account of the call of the first disciples (5:1–11). Jesus has been teaching all day beside the lake of Gennesaret, and the crowd has gotten so big that he gets claustrophobic, perhaps, and commandeers two fishing boats. He climbs into one of them, belonging to Peter, and they push out a little way from the shore. Not only does he have breathing room now, but water amplifies sound. Jesus finishes speaking to the crowd and then turns to the boat's impetuous owner and says, "Put out into the deep water and let down your nets for a catch" (Luke 5:4, NRSV).

Peter, no doubt rolling his eyes, says, "Master, we have worked all night long but have caught nothing. Yet if you say so, I will let down my nets." The results are spectacular. They haul up so many fish that their nets begin to break. Since nothing works quite like telling fishermen where to catch fish, Jesus also recruits his first three disciples on the spot, including James and John, the two sons (and probably only employees) at Zebedee and Sons Fishing Company, Inc. Nobody ever preaches this text from the father's perspective, but one can only imagine that he is not thrilled.

To be honest, there was nothing remarkable about the sermon. In my four decades in the pulpit, I have cranked out over a thousand sermons, and I remember a few of them. Those of us who try to have something to say week after week after week hope that, despite our limitations, something will get through. I was taught that preaching is not about saying what people "need to hear," but instead is an effort to get heard what it is that people need to say. One thing is certain. Our sermons are never as good, or as bad, as we think they are. To be honest, sometimes the best we can hope for is "Nice sermon, Reverend."

On this particular day that is not what I heard, however. A man about my age came through the line, and when we shook hands, he looked directly at me and said, "Reverend, I know where we can find some deep water."

Well, that was odd, I thought to myself. For a moment I was startled that it was actually a reference to the sermon, since most people leave them safely in the sanctuary. This particular man, who spoke fluent Spanish and was a frequent traveler to Central America, went on to describe what he meant by "deep water." He wanted to start a medical mission to the deaf community in Nicaragua. He had a good friend who was an audiologist, and they wanted to do something good in the second-poorest country in the Western Hemisphere. When I got my wits about me I said, "That sounds like deep water to me."

A small group of doctors and nurses in the church met and decided to make their first trip in 1999. At first we set up temporary clinics, did eye exams, and provided what assistance was possible before moving on to the next town. Then we decided to settle in one spot, a small town called Jinotega in the mountains of northern Nicaragua. We fell in love with the place, and with the people there. Because of grinding poverty, and perhaps a common antibiotic given by the Ministry of Health to treat ear infections with terrible unintended consequences, there are far too many deaf and hearing-impaired children in Nicaragua—not to mention adults who had never heard of an audiologist, much less seen one.

Our efforts were directed at establishing a permanent clinic and training Nicaraguan doctors. A local hospital allowed us to see patients in a nearby eye clinic, which ended up becoming our permanent home. In the twenty years since we first arrived, we have remodeled and equipped an ENT clinic in town, built audiology testing booths in several locations outside Jinotega, purchased and remodeled a house in Jinotega that is now a year-round boarding school for deaf students, started a commercial bakery that helps support the mission, added a computer lab, and begun partnering with Casa Materna, an organization that helps pregnant women.

We established a hearing screening program for all first graders in the community and now employ a permanent ENT doctor in Jinotega. We took over management of an international hearing aid purchase consortium and in 2014 launched the first audiometry training and certification program in the country. The old, rambling house that we renovated in the center of town is called the Albergue Mayflower (the Mayflower Inn). Twenty-five children now live there, along with a staff of teachers and custodians. Its credo is simple: *Either all of us matter, or none of us do.*

In the years since the words "deep water" were first uttered in a sanctuary on the red dirt of Oklahoma, over 150 volunteers have served the Mayflower Medical Outreach (MMO)—doctors, nurses, translators, deaf educators, audiologists, medical researchers, speech therapists, artists, adult and youth ministers, and parishioners who did general construction. All because of a puff of air turned loose in a sanctuary? Can a minister flapping his lips in Oklahoma cause a medical mission miracle in Nicaragua?

The words of Isaiah come to mind: "For as the rain and the snow come down from heaven, and do not return there until they have watered the earth, making it bring forth and sprout, giving seed to the sower and bread to the eater, so shall my word be that goes out from my mouth; *it shall not return to me empty, but it shall accomplish that which I purpose, and succeed in the thing for which I sent it*" (Isaiah 55:10–11, NRSV, emphasis mine).

As I write, a photograph of our first three graduates from public high school in Jinotega has just arrived on my computer. Three smiling young men in their caps and gowns. They look like any other high school graduates except that they are deaf, and they would never have made it without the program we established. They plan to go on to college because they can communicate. Now they have a real chance—not only at a decent life but to inspire others. This is the hope that Emily Dickinson described as "the thing with feathers— / That perches in the soul— / And sings the tune without the words— / And never stops—at all."

That thing is God, but it's not a thing at all. This God can network the whole universe. How else can so little good do so much good? How else could a pinch of leaven have corrupted the loaf of the empire? How else could two words in an ordinary sermon have given birth to such an extraordinary mission? This God does not have to suspend natural law to make a miracle. The nature of creation itself is miraculous. This God does not need to do special favors for chosen people, pulling strings. This God is the string. A God who does not discriminate but is the "strange attractor" of chaos theory itself. A God of incomprehensible, universal equilibrium. Not a distant God, but a God who could not be closer.

This is the God in whom "we live, and move, and have our being." The unbearable lightness of being. When Jesus of Nazareth told his friends, "My peace I leave with you," he wasn't leaving instructions. He was leaving himself. Not at a molecular level but at a *quantum* level. It worked. If you doubt it, then just do something good today for goodness' sake, and then forget about it.

Everything may look the same tomorrow, but everything will be different. How will you know? You won't. But you will *trust* in the power of the Luminous Web. The deeper and wider that trust becomes, the more generous your spirit will become. The more generous your spirit becomes, the more wastefully you will love. The more wastefully you love, the more compassionately you will live. The more compassionately you live, the more deeply and authentically you will forgive.

Then and only then will you realize that an old saying has it exactly backward. *No good deed goes unpunished.* I've heard this aphorism all my life. It's clever, but there is just one small problem with it. It's not true.

A good deed is a good deed regardless of whether you can calculate its ultimate effect, so be careful not to think only of yourself in the short term. In a world of spiritual entanglement, that old saying, like religion itself, needs revision: *No good deed goes unrewarded.*

All it takes is a deep and stubborn trust in the Luminous

Web. But be careful. If you start acting under the influence of unconditional love, and you give it away as freely as it has been given to you, there is a chance that someone will use an old, old name to describe you. It might be the last thing you thought anybody would ever call you.

A *believer*.

Notes

Prologue:
The Night God Fell from the Ceiling

1. "Pietro Bonatti, Caretaker of Sistine Chapel, Is Dead," *The New York Times*, May 23, 1972.

2. Jana Reiss, "Why Millennials Are Really Leaving Religion (It's Not Just Politics, Folks)," *Religion News Service*, June 26, 2018, https://religionnews.com/2018/06/26/why-millennials-are-really -leaving-religion-its-not-just-politics-folks/.

3. Reiss, "Why Millennials Are Really Leaving Religion."

1:
Made in the Image of Humans

1. Barbara Brown Taylor used this surpassingly beautiful name for God in a book by the same title, *The Luminous Web: Essays on Science and Religion* (Cambridge, MA: Cowley Publications, 2000). The theft is born of both admiration and envy. At Mayflower these days, the most common name for God besides "God" is "the Luminous Web."

2. J. S. Spong, *A New Christianity for a New World: Why Traditional Faith Is Dying & How a New Faith Is Being Born* (San Francisco: HarperSanFrancisco, 2001), p. 38.

3. Sir Edward Burnett Tylor, *Primitive Culture: Researches into the Development of Mythology, Philosophy, Religion, Art, and Custom* (London: J. Murray, 1871), p. 260.

4.   Spong, *A New Christianity*, p. 45.

5.   Robert Banks, *And Man Created God: Is God a Human Invention?* (Oxford: Lion Hudson, 2011), p. 45.

6.   Banks, *And Man Created God*, p. 42.

7.   See Andrew Newberg, Eugene D'Aquili, and Vince Rause, *Why God Won't Go Away: Brain Science and the Biology of Belief* (New York: Ballantine Books, 2001).

8.   Adapted from a story by Fred B. Craddock, *Craddock Stories*, ed. Mike Graves and Richard Ward (St. Louis: Chalice Press, 2001), p. 21.

9.   Catherine Keller, *On the Mystery: Discerning Divinity in Process* (Minneapolis: Fortress Press, 2008), p. xiii.

10.   Andee-Sue Clark, "Significance of the Tearing of the Temple Curtain," *Verbum* 10, no. 1 (2012), http://fisherpub.sjfc.edu/verbum/vol10/iss1/14.

11.   Paul Tillich explores this concept in all his work, including *The Shaking of the Foundations*.

2:
Quantum Physics and the Common Good

1.   From the introduction of Michelle Bamberger and Robert Oswald's *The Real Cost of Fracking* (New York: Penguin Random House, 2015).

2.   Notes from an interview over dinner at the Shed restaurant, Kingfisher, Oklahoma, Friday, February 1, 2019, with Abbie and Lamar Ashley.

3.   Barbara Brown Taylor, *The Luminous Web: Essays on Science and Religion* (Cambridge, MA: Cowley Publications, 2000), p. 9.

4.   For a complete and disturbing account of intra-Christian violence, see Philip Jenkins, *The Jesus Wars: How Four Patriarchs, Three Queens, and Two Emperors Decided What Christians Would Believe for the Next 1,500 Years* (New York: HarperOne, 2010).

5.   Stephen Hawking, *A Brief History of Time* (New York: Bantam Books, 1988), p. 175.

6. Taylor, *Luminous Web*, pp. 37–39, used with permission.

7. For an excellent introduction to this famous experiment, see Arthur Fine, "The Einstein-Podolsky-Rosen Argument in Quantum Theory," *The Stanford Encyclopedia of Philosophy* (Winter 2017 edition), ed. Edward N. Zalta, https://plato.stanford.edu/archives /win2017/entries/qt-epr/.

8. Taylor, *Luminous Web*, p. 55.

9. "The Chirp Heard Across the Universe" (editorial), *The New York Times*, February 16, 2016.

3:
Sin as the Illusion That We Are Home Alone

1. Quoted in "What About Sin?" ProgressiveChristianity.org, no date, https://progressivechristianity.org/resources/what-about-sin/.

2. Matthew Fox, *Sins of the Spirit, Blessings of the Flesh: Lessons for Transforming Evil in Self and Society* (New York: Harmony Books, 1999).

3. Raymond Tallis, *Newton's Sleep: The Two Cultures and the Two Kingdoms* (New York: St. Martin's Press, 1995), p. 79.

4. Tom Boyd, *Lusting for Infinity: A Spiritual Odyssey* (Norman, OK: Line-in, 2015), pp. 56–57.

5. Boyd, *Lusting for Infinity*, p. 57.

4:
Faith as Trust, Not Belief

1. Essay by Emilee Bounds, June 30, 2017.

2. Elaine Pagels, *Beyond Belief: The Secret Gospel of Thomas* (New York: Vintage Books, 2004), p. 5.

3. Pagels, *Beyond Belief*, p. 9.

4. Rodney Stark, *The Rise of Christianity: A Sociologist Reconsiders History* (Princeton, NJ: Princeton University Press, 1996), pp. 86–87.

5. Marcus Borg, *Days of Awe and Wonder: How to Be a Christian in the 21st Century* (New York: HarperOne, 2017), pp. 21–22.

6. Ken Wilber, *One Taste: Daily Reflections on Integral Spirituality* (Boston & London: Shambhala, 2000), p. 34.

7. Borg, *Days of Awe and Wonder*, p. 28.

8. Borg, *Days of Awe and Wonder*, p. 30.

9. "A Christmas Memory" was originally published in *Mademoiselle* magazine in December 1956, reprinted in *The Selected Writings of Truman Capote* in 1963, and issued as a stand-alone hardcover edition by Random House in 1966.

5:
Prayer as Access, Not Petition

1. John Dominic Crossan, *The Greatest Prayer: Rediscovering the Revolutionary Message of the Lord's Prayer* (New York: HarperOne, 2010), p. 1.

2. Crossan, *Greatest Prayer*, p. 15.

3. Susannah Heschel, *Abraham Joshua Heschel: Essential Writings* (Maryknoll, NY: Orbis Books, 2011), p. 137.

4. Crossan, *Greatest Prayer*, p. 20.

5. Heschel, *Abraham Joshua Heschel*, p. 145.

6. Heschel, *Abraham Joshua Heschel*.

7. Crossan, *Greatest Prayer*, p. 28.

8. Fred B. Craddock, *Overhearing the Gospel* (Nashville: Abingdon, 1978), pp. 105–6.

9. Crossan, *Greatest Prayer*, p. 28.

10. Diana Butler Bass, *Grounded: Finding God in the World* (New York: HarperOne, 2015), p. 228.

11. Bass, *Grounded*, p. 228.

6:
Every Move We Make: A Theology of Consequence

1. Barbara Brown Taylor, *The Luminous Web: Essays on Science and Religion* (Cambridge, MA: Cowley Publications, 2000), pp. 94–95.

2.   Lily Rothman and Arpita Aneja, "You Still Don't Know the Whole Rosa Parks Story," *Time*, November 30, 2015, http://time.com/4125377/rosa-parks-60-years-video/.

3.   Taylor, *Luminous Web*, p. 96.

4.   Edward B. Davis, "Debating Darwin: The 'Intelligent Design' Movement," *The Christian Century* (July 15–22, 1998), p. 681.

5.   George Johnson, *Fire in the Mind* (New York: Vintage Books, 1995), p. 96. Quoted in Taylor, *Luminous Web*, p. 96.

6.   Taylor, *Luminous Web*, p. 33.

7.   James Baldwin, *Fifty Famous People: A Book of Short Stories* (New York: American Book Company, 1912), pp. 51–54.

8.   Taylor, *Luminous Web*, p. 98.

9.   Diana Butler Bass, *Grounded: Finding God in the World* (New York: HarperOne, 2015), p. 4.

10.   For a good introduction to Process Theology, read John B. Cobb, Jr., and David Ray Griffin's *Process Theology: An Introductory Exposition* (Louisville: Westminster John Knox Press, 1976).

11.   W. Somerset Maugham, *The Summing Up* (Garden City, NY: Doubleday, 1938), pp. 87–88.

12.   Adapted from a story by Fred B. Craddock, *Craddock Stories*, ed. Mike Graves and Richard Ward (St. Louis: Chalice Press, 2001), pp. 24–25.

7:
The Center of the Universe

1.   Marcus Borg, *Days of Awe and Wonder: How to Be a Christian in the 21st Century* (New York: HarperOne, 2017), pp. 37–38.

2.   Martin Luther King, Jr., *Letter from Birmingham Jail*, April 16, 1963.

3.   This parable received the highest number of red votes of any parable among the participants of the Jesus Seminar. See Brandon Scott, *Re-imagine the World: An Introduction to the Parables of Jesus* (Santa Rosa, CA: Polebridge Press, 2001), p. 21.

4.　Art Dewey, "A Death That Would Not Die: A Primer on Jesus and the Passion" (lecture, Westar Institute meeting, Santa Rosa, California, Spring 2018).

5.　Paul Davies, *God and the New Physics* (New York: Simon & Schuster, 1983), p. 112.

6.　C. A. Hilgartner, Martha A. Bartter, and Ronald V. Harrington, "We Must Also Eliminate Peace," https://hilgart.org/papers/071S188 .512.html.

7.　See Kathleen Corley, *Maranatha: Women's Funerary Rituals and Christian Origins* (Minneapolis: Fortress Press, 2010).

8.　Adapted from a sermon by Fred Craddock, recorded in Halifax, Nova Scotia, 1983.

Epilogue:
Above Us Only Sky

1.　Imtiaz Ahmad, "Pakistani School Drops John Lennon's Imagine from Concert After Protest," *Hindustan Times*, August 25, 2017, https://www.hindustantimes.com/world-news/pakistani-school -drops-john-lennon-s-imagine-from-concert-after-protest/story -NDm8TvtsUN81nLyQy5ooTL.html.

2.　https://www.goodreads.com/quotes/112387-i-believe-in-god -but-not-as-one-thing-not.

3.　Jordan Michael Smith, "Stop Imagining," *The American Conservative*, December 2, 2010.

4.　Joni Mitchell, "Woodstock," *Ladies of the Canyon*, 1970.

5.　Richard Rohr, *The Universal Christ: How a Forgotten Reality Can Change Everything We See, Hope for, and Believe* (New York: Convergent, 2019), pp. 6–7.

Acknowledgments

There are no self-made human beings, and no solitary authors who write books. All of us who are lucky enough to do this work know that we are surrounded—not only by a cloud of witnesses but also by a host of co-conspirators. A very special word of thanks goes to Roger Freet, my former editor and now agent, who would not let me off the hook until this book was the best it could be. In particular, he pushed me toward a pastoral, narrative tone of voice, lest this be just another tedious argument for or against the existence of God. It took forever, Roger, but it was worth it.

For my editor, Derek Reed, whose aggressive use of the delete button saved me from sounding as flaky as I am, and who made the book easier to read and understand. For Hilary Roberts and the amazing copy editors at Penguin Random House who see all the little things that authors miss, saving us from embarrassment. And for all the people I have not met, and will never meet, whose work in the actual production of any book is often hidden from view. Someone is, after all, cleaning up the offices in the middle of the night, and running the presses, and driving the trucks that deliver the work of our hands into the hands of others—all so that we will never forget that there is no artifact as beautiful as a book, nor a blessing as powerful or irreplaceable as reading.

For the writing of Barbara Brown Taylor, whose book *The Luminous Web* was the egg that hatched into this book, and for my mentor and teacher Fred Craddock, who was the shortest giant of a storyteller I ever heard in the pulpit.

For my beloved congregation, the Good Ship Mayflower, where I have served amazing and wonderful people for thirty-five years, and whose stories fill this book with light and wisdom. And last, but an eternity from least, for my wife, Shawn, an extraordinary artist and teacher, who not only has given me the gift of children and grandchildren, but whose love keeps me grounded. When a book is being written in our house, she knows that I go away to a far country, and her patience and support until I return is pure grace—which in the end is all that can save us.

About the Author

Rev. Robin R. Meyers is senior minister of Mayflower Congregational UCC church of Oklahoma City, and Distinguished Professor of Social Justice Emeritus in the Philosophy Department at Oklahoma City University. He is the author of seven previous books about religion and culture, including the national bestseller *Saving Jesus from the Church: How to Stop Worshiping Christ and Start Following Jesus.* A newspaper columnist and commentator for National Public Radio, Dr. Meyers lectures nationally and internationally on the merits of Progressive Christianity and seeks to recover faith as the embodied and radical compassion of a Beloved Community. This work is now the subject of a feature-length documentary film entitled *American Heretics: The Politics of the Gospel* (www.americanhereticsthefilm.com).

He is married to Shawn Meyers, an artist and professor, and they are the parents of three children, Blue, Chelsea, and Cass, and now grandparents to three amazing granddaughters, Iris, Hazel, and Eleanora.

About the Type

This book was set in Berling. Designed in 1951 by Karl-Erik Forsberg (1914–95) for the type foundry Berlingska Stilgjuteri AB in Lund, Sweden, it was released the same year in foundry type by H. Berthold AG. A classic old-face design, its generous proportions and inclined serifs make it highly legible.